Having the privilege of rea... ... answer to my prayers. This ... rut I'm in and how to live ... nudge" I so desperately need... also shown me a more positi... am eternally grateful. Thank you so much for a way to change my life for the better.

- Stacie Bailey, Fairview, OR

"*Once I started reading it I could not stop.... From the beginning I felt as if I was reading about my life. As I read more I realized I am not alone in the way I feel and think. Then I started to see other people that I know in this book also, and the everyday problems they complain about.* Simple Steps for Real Life *is a fantastic book that people should take the time to read, and if they are honest with themselves, they will see what aspects in their life they need to work on to have a happier, stress free life style.*

- D. Clemens, Owensboro, KY

From the very start of (this book) I felt emotion "well up" inside of me. I know that being privileged to read Simple Steps for Real Life *was the gentle nudge I have needed. Whatever life may be presenting you with at the moment, by reading* Simple Steps for Real Life *you too can realize that starting over is liberating. We do all have our own answers within and we can create the life of our dreams by starting with a first step-a simple step! Thank you so very much, Cheryl! I am now ready to get to the heart of my soul!*

- Helen Brewster Henderson, Prestatyn, North Wales, UK

I love that Cheryl writes from personal experiences and the wisdom she has gained over the years. She deals with deep emotions and situations to building confidence and finding your true nature. Cheryl has a wonderful flare to give simple steps and practical solutions that can bring real change to anyone's life. If you wish to change and live the life you dream of, this is the book for you! - Flower Overton, Hampshire, UK

Authentic. Genuine. Caring. These are the words that come to mind over and over again through Cheryl Maloney's incredible book, Simple Steps for Real Life. *Cheryl gives us a veritable pathway to happiness as she systematically illuminates a way through the maze of possible life challenges. She writes from the soul and we know immediately that she has known pain, she has known anxiety and stress yet came through trials to the other side. She is now an expert in pain control! Rarely does a book give us a formula for great results in so few pages. It is without hesitation that I recommend* Simple Steps for Real Life *and know that it will be by your side for many years to come.*

- Mary Cimiluca, Executive Producer, Viktor & I,
An Alexander Vesely Film

Firstly, it is refreshing and even uplifting to know that those of us who come to that fork in the road where staying in a rut is much easier than rising above it, aren't alone. Simple Steps for Real Life *gives everyone the blueprint to live their best life on their own terms. Following it will show anyone willing to do the work that they are never too old and it is never too late to be true to who they are supposed to be.* Simple Steps for Real Life *certainly makes achieving personal goals and happiness seem within anyone's reach if they will work for it. I'm in!*

- Katie B., Las Vegas, NV

From an older person's perspective I can identify with Cheryl's dynamic advice. Most interesting because our life experiences teach us to grow. However not all individuals think the same way. Many will not think of looking at life's experiences as growth or a learning tool, which make us stronger; too many individuals often take a different path and continue to make the same mistakes. I applaud Cheryl for the courage to take charge of her life. It is just as important for her to share and try to help others with what she has learned from her own experiences.

-   Gloria M. Hernandez, San Antonio, TX

-

What I loved most about reading Simple Steps for Real Life *was knowing that I am not alone in feeling the way I have when I have experienced a bump in the road called Life. I believe I am a very positive person, however even a person with a positive attitude can often be very hard on one's self when mistakes are made. I enjoyed the real advice and tips that Cheryl provided when deciding to pursue one's dreams. What I learned from Cheryl that I had really not thought about before was how I react to things in my life is really my choice, whether it be a reaction to a positive or negative experience in my life, I control my attitude and ultimately my reaction to the experiences of my life. I look forward to sharing with my family and friends the positive outcomes I know I will experience from putting Cheryl's advice into practice. By sharing with those that I love, I hope to continue to pay forward the happiness that Cheryl inspires us to feel and to live with a thankful heart!*

-Jenee Margo Gonzales, San Antonio, TX

I have so many feelings that I don't know which one to say first. My life is listed in almost all of the steps. Simple Steps for Real Life *made me think of so many things that I can change in my life to be happier. Plus ways to do it. This book will be a life saver to many people.... Cheryl makes hopes and dreams realities....*

- S. Teagarden, Sarasota, FL

-

I was immediately drawn in by the simple and straightforward style of Simple Steps for Real Life. *Few times have I felt as if an author was actually able to speak to me and as if they were me at the same time. I have so often felt exactly what Cheryl was describing and her description of her journey makes it easy to connect.* Simple Steps *delivers just that, a simple common sense approach to problem solving with solutions that are easily applied to your daily life, as well as to your larger life goals and most importantly very clearly gives you advice on HOW to do it.* Simple Steps for Real Life *is a guide for life, not just a book and Cheryl is the perfect Sherpa to help deliver you back to a more well balanced and fulfilled life! Thank you Cheryl for helping to shift my view!*

- H. Madsen

Simple Steps
for
Real Life

Also by Cheryl L. Maloney

Simple Steps Real Change, the Book
Simple Inspirations
Simple Inspirations Journal
Life, Simply
Finding Peace, Simply
Inspirational Resource Compendium
Simple Steps for Starting Over (Later in Life) 8/2012

Simple Steps
for
Real Life

By Cheryl Maloney

Published by Simple Steps... Real Change

Second Edition. Revised and updated July 2012
ISBN: 10-1478174498
ISBN 13-9781478174493
Library of Congress Control Number: 2011961498

Printed in the United States of America
Self-Published rev. date: 07/04/2012

Your time is limited so don't waste it living someone else's life. Don't be trapped by dogma — which is living with the results of other people's thinking.

Don't let the noise of others' opinions drown out your own inner voice.

And most important, have the courage to follow your heart and intuition. They somehow already know what you want to become. Everything else is secondary.

—Steve Jobs

Simple Steps for Real Life

This book is dedicated to Jack, my husband of thirty-three years, who has stood by me through the good times and the not so good. Who has encouraged me to step up and into my dreams. He is the love of my life and my best friend. ILYJ

Preface

In your hands, you are holding the culmination of two years of focusing on how to make life simply better. We all go through times when we wonder "Why is this happening to me?" ... yet the answers seem to elude us.

The stresses of this modern day world take their toll on each of us. I know. I've allowed that to happen to me in the past ... and sometimes it still does. The good news is we can take a **Simple Step**, a slight shift in our perspective, our attitude, our energy ... and we can change our world.

I truly believe that life is meant to be happy. And while we may go through challenges, pain and suffering ... those experiences lead us to a different place. The question becomes whether we let it define us, destroy us or strengthen us. For me it is the latter.

Each one of us gets to make our own choice ... and it's a choice about how to live our life. Our attitude is a choice, too.

For me, **Simple** is the key to affecting change in our lives. Why? Because everyone can take a **Simple Step**. You only have to take one ... and then repeat it ... until it becomes a habit. By focusing on just that one step, you master it, gaining the confidence to take another one.

This is all about what works for you. Some steps won't ... others might not be easy. You get to choose where to start and what step to take.

You are not alone ... I am here. Take my hand ... Turn the page! Let's take a **Simple Step** together.

Cheryl Maloney
Portland, Oregon
2012

Table of Contents

Part I: Know It! Tune Into You

Part II: Release It! Let It Go

Part III: Own It! Take Responsibility

Part IV: Choose It! You Have Choices

Part V: Desire It! Know What You Want

Part VI: See It! Visualize

Part VII: Give It! Be Thankful

Forward

You are about to begin an amazing adventure that you were destined for. A journey that will unlock your inner yearnings, help you open the door to your heart's desire and gently move you towards the life you were meant to live - the life the world now needs you to embrace.

Simple Steps for Real Life is more of a road map then just another motivational book, and it was written by a person who lived it before she wrote it. A person who speaks from the heart but also speaks from the trenches. And a person who knows about the twists and turns and valleys and mountain tops because her path, like ours, has been filled with joys and challenges and hopes and fears.

Imagine having your own personal GPS programmed with the voice of a warm, wise and gentle woman ready to guide you turn-by-turn in a reliable and encouraging way. A voice that's clear and direct and takes you one step at a time towards a life that's not only possible and real, but one that is also joyful, authentic and fulfilling! The life you were destined to have.

You must be ready to begin because you are here ... I wish you the journey of a lifetime!

Godspeed,

Paul Boynton

Acknowledgements

To every person who has come to **Simple Steps . . . Real Change** and who spreads the ripples of positivity far and wide. I am grateful for your friendship and your love. You are a constant source of inspiration . . . and you always give me hope!

Kenny Brixey, my friend and business partner. It is because of Kenny's wisdom and experience as a life coach that we are taking **Simple Steps** beyond the words on the page and into **Real Life**. He is my beacon, infusing my life with light.

Nancy Luscombe, who started out as my editor and became my friend and confidant. Nancy makes me a better writer, a better communicator . . . and a better person.

Brent Carey, the power behind *Empower Radio*, who saw in me what I didn't realize was there. He lives his passion by shepherding in a new era where positive press will replace network news.

Paul Boynton, author of *Begin with Yes* and CEO of Moore Center Service. As a friend and role model to me . . . Paul shows me what real altruism means.

Mary Cimiluca, Entrepreneur and Executive Producer of the film *Viktor & I*. My friend, my role model . . . the person who knows to push me forward when I hesitate.

Introduction

We are all looking for a way to lead a better life. Whether financially, romantically or overall quality of life … we want life to be everything we want it to be. And we want it to be, well … simple! At least that is what I believe….

When I first started writing a blog in 2009, it was my therapy, my solace. I was an out-of-work, out-of-shape, over-fifty corporate executive collecting unemployment, questioning my own worth, dealing with my husband Jack's scary health diagnoses and beating myself up for the stupid financial mistakes I had made. Is that enough baggage?

After months of writing daily, I started posting my thoughts on Facebook. I knew I wasn't alone in my challenges … but I soon realized how many people were dealing with major issues in their lives – just like me. Within eighteen months our **Simple Steps** posts were viewed, shared and quoted over fifty million times!

Are you sick and tired of living a life that doesn't meet your own expectations? Do you feel unfulfilled and have no idea how to move from where you are to where you want to be? That's where I was and why I've written this book for you. We can do this! My dream is to help you realize a happy life … on your terms and as simply as possible.

There is no complex plan, expensive program or sage wisdom required. It takes only one small change in perspective, in attitude or in action to change your life. Within you is everything you need to create your dream life. We, however, let life get in the way of our dreams, and it takes a gentle nudge to enable us to see clearly.

Simple Steps for Real Life is that gentle nudge. Whether you need to move past your past, learn to trust your own instincts or break out of a rut, it takes only the smallest action to make a huge difference. And that's what I'm going to show you how to do! It's up to you to decide if you are ready to move forward. This is about you, your real life and your choice.

Simple Steps for Real Life enables you to work on what you want to,
including:

Know It! Tune Into You—Helps you figure out what is really
important to you.

Release It! Let It Go—Encourages you to break a cycle that's keeping
you from moving forward in confidence.

Own It! Take Responsibility—Lets you know it's your life and it's
in your control. Know it and take it!

Choose It! You Have Choices—Enables you to see through the
clutter and realize you get to decide what works for you in every situation.

Desire It! Know What You Want—Digs deep to help you realize what
your passion is . . . what makes your heart sing and your soul speak.

See It! Visualize—When you can see your dreams, you can live
them.

Give It! Be Thankful—Sincere gratitude opens your life up to even more to
be grateful for.

If you truly want to start over, the chapters are organized to help you step on
solid ground. Start at the beginning and follow it through, or focus on what
you want. With knowledge, choices and action, you will get to the heart of
you, deal with what holds you back and pursue the life of your dreams. It's
all up to you.

It's **Simple**! So let's move forward and create the **Real Life** of your
dreams!

KNOW IT!

TUNE INTO YOU

You have to leave the city of your comfort and go into
the wilderness of your intuition.
What you'll discover will be wonderful.
What you'll discover is yourself.

– Alan Alda

Know It! Tune Into You
Introduction

There comes a time when we need to stand on our own two feet. For some, this may have happened early on when, as a child, that independent streak came across loud and clear. For others, perhaps it came later in life when the ones they relied upon for guidance were no longer around. And then there are folks like me.

I always thought I was the good daughter … the one who did whatever my parents told me to do. But one day when I was talking to Gordon, a good friend of my Dad's, I made that comment, and he just laughed. He said that wasn't the girl he knew at all … and then added that I was rather "spirited." Somewhere between childhood and becoming an adult, I seem to have lost that part of me, and I'm not sure how or why.

At some point in our lives, we begin to question our decisions: a mistake, a series of failed relationships, one bad financial decision after another, jobs that didn't suit us and even friends that we learned we couldn't trust. We start adding up all our "failings" and decide that someone else has better judgment than we do. For example, I decided there had to be a better way to prepare for retirement than working nine to five. I attended seminars, bought books and even participated in coaching from noted "gurus." I invested my retirement savings, purchased investment properties and funneled every spare dollar I had into the then-hot real estate market. The entire time I had a pit in my stomach, and red flags were waving in front of my eyes. But I ignored my own gut feelings because I felt someone else knew better than I did. In doing so I ended up losing everything I'd invested in, and at age fifty-four, I hit rock bottom.

The good news is that rock bottom is solid ground. I came to a place where I learned some really hard lessons, and it was in that knowledge that I found my voice. That's how I came to be here … writing about *Simple Steps for Real Life*. More importantly, I came to realize that my instincts are the best resource I have.

3

Sure, there are times when we need expert advice. But that's what it is … advice. Only we can decide what is right for us. When we tune into ourselves, we make the decision to hear our own soul. It takes some practice - especially if we've relied on others more than we've relied on ourselves.

As you go through the **Simple Steps** in this chapter, you're going to learn about finding the time to be still and exercise self-care. In that space you'll learn how to hear your own voice and trust your instincts.

As you gain confidence in yourself, it will be time to face your own truths and decide what works for you and what doesn't. That knowledge may come in the form of self-examination or from dealing with roadblocks, naysayers and setbacks. We learn from every step of our journey … but we learn more when we overcome adversity. It is through this process that we not only gain strength, but we also recognize what we already possess.

Tuning into yourself also necessitates dealing with worries and fears, and that can be scary - especially if you've never let them see the light of day. The funny thing about fear is, when you expose it to the light, it's not as scary as you first thought. We tend to give negative experiences more attention than they deserve. If your worry arises from past mistakes or issues, I'll show you how to redirect your focus to your successes - you've probably had many more of those than you are giving yourself credit for! When you see your experience in a better light, taking that leap of faith forward becomes a natural step!

Get excited about moving to your new reality, and that passion will carry you forward and turn your dreams into real life!

If you're ready to get to the heart of your soul … turn the page. Tune into you!

4

Find Objectivity

How many times have you experienced an event in your life that turned out to be a blessing in disguise? Or … what you thought was going to be the best thing for you ended up not being so good?

Rather than labeling our experiences good or bad, what if we look at them more objectively? I know … when it comes to our own lives, it's not so easy to be objective. The question we have to ask ourselves is this: do we want a positive or a negative outcome? That helps determine our course of action.

When you need help finding an objective assessment of your own personal challenges, here are a few **Simple Steps** to give you some much-needed perspective.

- Stand back and become an observer of your life. If what is transpiring in your life was happening to your best friend, what advice would you give? Would you be objective and help your friend work through the challenge? When we are too close to a stressful situation, it's very difficult to be objective. If, however, we take a step back and take the time to process in our mind and heart what is happening, we can deal with it more effectively.

- Don't allow yourself to be rushed into making a decision. Unless we are talking about life or death situations, there is nothing that requires you to act immediately. This situation comes up often when someone is trying to convince you to buy their product or service. On a personal level, pressure to do or not do something "for" someone or "for" the relationship should be a big red flag. Take the time to analyze how important the decision is to your life. When you make a decision, it has to be right for you, not for someone else. In personal relationships you are only responsible for your life, your happiness and your well being.

- Create a Pro/Con list. This is another exercise that should not be rushed. Take the time to consider each side of the decision to be made. What are the immediate and longer term impacts? When you feel you've created a comprehensive list, it's time to determine what matters most to you. Go somewhere that you won't be disturbed or influenced. As you glance over your list, cross out anything you just don't care about. What remains? At this point you have boiled down the list to what matters to you, and you can make a thoughtful decision.

I'd suggest that we add in one more criteria to our chosen result: make it a win-win for everyone. That just feels better.

When we learn to be more objective about our own lives, we cease to get caught up in the drama of life's challenges. When we are not stressed and learn to enjoy the journey, we're happier. What is better than that!?!

Know Your Strengths

On any given day we can go through a range of emotions from ecstatic to depressed. Things happen that we don't understand and are not prepared for, and they trigger our reactions. There might even be a person in our life – a spouse, a parent, maybe even a boss – who, with a single word, can cut us to the core.

It would be easy to say, "Just ignore them." But that isn't realistic. If, however, you have a strong sense of self, those situations are easier to deal with.

So, how exactly do you get to that point? The point where you hear what they have to say, but you don't let it impact how you feel about yourself.

You know in your heart the type of person you are. You know what's important to you, you know right from wrong, and most of all, you know you're a good person. When you have those core beliefs as your foundation, you hold the key to dealing with any issue that comes your way. It does, however, take the desire to focus on your positive qualities ... especially if you're taking grief from someone who matters to you.

Try these **Simple Steps** to build your strong foundation:

- Start by identifying your strengths. Make a list - a comprehensive list. This should include everything you know you're good at, down to some of the more fundamental skills you have. For example: at one end of the spectrum you might have "calming influence" or "good under pressure" while at the other end you may include "good list maker" "careful shopper" or "great baker." By being all-encompassing about your strengths, you can pull them out and use them when you run into a stressful situation.

- How, you ask, does being a careful shopper help you when your boss is criticizing your work? You draw upon your attention to detail such as reading labels (getting all the facts), comparing prices

7

(understanding cost effective measures) and only purchasing when it makes sense (making an informed decision).

- When you are faced with criticism, listen to what is being said … then walk away. That will give you the time to process the intent, not just the words. If you can't walk away, ask for a few minutes to think through what the person has said. The key here is taking the time to deal with it, rather than simply reacting to it. Take this time to draw on your strengths. Identify which ones will serve you in this situation. Use them.

The beauty of these **Simple Steps** is that you begin from a foundation of what you are good at. When you focus on the positive aspects of your life, you know you can handle anything that comes your way.

When You're Scared

There are times in our lives when we face uncertainly ... sometimes it's downright scary. Perhaps everything we thought we knew changed, or there's something totally out of our experience, and we don't know where to begin. We need help but don't know where to turn. A miracle would be nice.

Being afraid doesn't come with limits. What worries you may be inconsequential to someone else. For example: one person facing foreclosure may be fearful about losing their home. Another person may have hit rock bottom and losing their home is a burden they need lifted.

It's easy to get stuck in a place of worry and fear.

No one gets to tell us what we should or shouldn't worry about. What's important though is the realization that worrying doesn't make it better. Worrying uses up the creative and resourceful energy we need to move past our fears.

Here's a good example from my life. My husband, Jack, was diagnosed with cancer. While the doctors were working on a treatment plan, we didn't know what that would involve or how he would be affected. It would have been easy to get stuck in a place of worry and fear. But that wouldn't have changed anything.

In times like these we need to draw from our inner soul and find some peace. When we ground ourselves, we give ourselves the gift of both time and perspective. No ... it's not easy ... but it's simple.

To move out of fear and find your center, try one of these **Simple Steps**:

- Find a quiet place and breathe deeply. Try yoga, mediation or any practice that calms you. In this **Simple Step** the point is to clear out distractions. There is time to consult, research and even seek comfort, but this isn't it.

- Take the time to determine what the true fear is. Worrying creates an abundance of secondary thoughts. Boil it down to what is the biggest concern. For example: "Where will I live?" or "Is this life threatening?" When you get to the root of your concerns, the focus is clear.

- Seek expert counsel. I love the Internet, but sometimes it's hard to distinguish between credible experts and junk. Local consumer bureaus, medical and legal boards, community service centers and the Better Business Bureau have resources to explore. Make an appointment. Most experts offer free or low cost consultations. If you choose to ask a friend for a reference, make sure it's someone whose judgment you trust.

When we are most afraid is the time we need to be the most calm, methodical and patient. It isn't easy ... however, when you take yourself to this better place, you'll realize you can deal with whatever comes your way. And that is power.

Your New Reality

Life changing events happen in everyone's lives and cannot be ignored or swept under the carpet. Death of a loved one, illness or scary diagnosis, job loss, loss of a home, divorce or the end of a significant relationship - when these occur, it's important to recognize that you have to travel the road that goes with them. There are no detours or magic erasers that enable you to move past them unaffected.

There may be guilt, anger, fear, panic and hopelessness associated with these powerful events. Acknowledge those feelings and don't let anyone tell you to "get over it." The key is to realize that you're going through a type of grieving ... we all deal with it differently.

Be kind to yourself. Give yourself time to adjust to your new reality. For some this might take a day, a week, a month or more - perhaps even longer. When that time is over, make a commitment to take a **Simple Step** forward in your new life. One note here ... grieving over a significant loss is not a once and done thing. Recognize that you may still have moments that put you into a tailspin. The important thing is to have a plan on how to regain control and rise up again.

Here are a few **Simple Steps** to help you in your recovery:

- Decide what you want your life to be like going forward. For example: if you have lost your job, perhaps you'll decide to go back to school and start a new career. If you have lost someone close, you might decide that just being able to laugh again is your first step. Stock up on funny movies to give yourself an escape from your loss. Note: this doesn't mean you're trying to forget your loss. It means you're giving your brain a small break - just enough to feel a little bit better. Baby steps....

- Start a gratitude journal and write in it every day. This helps you focus on what you have rather than what you don't have. Carry it with you and add to it as something comes to mind. As you write, take a minute to acknowledge the feeling that comes to mind. For example: if you are grateful that your children are there to support you, note the love you feel for each one of them. Later, when you reread your journal, you will experience both the gratitude and love again.

- Seek out a partner to help you. Whether a trusted friend or relative, ask them to be your sounding board and also your grounding board. A grounding board is the person who gently reminds you that it's time to come back up out of your sorrow. For example, if you are dealing with the end of a relationship and you see your ex out with someone else, it's going to affect you. When you call or cry to your grounding board, they hear you out and remind you that your ex wasn't the right person for you. You deserve to be your partner's top priority and you weren't.

You have to do what is right for you ... no one walks in your shoes. When, however, you choose to move forward in your life, having a plan to help yourself is a **Simple Step** in the direction of your new dreams. Take it. It just feels better!

Are You Listening?

For much of my life I was a person who always had to be in control. When something went wrong … I had to do something about it. I would take matters into my own hands, whether it was to write a letter, call someone, rearrange the chairs or organize the lives of everyone around me!

All the while I was doing this, however, a little voice in the back of my head was telling me to chill out, be quiet … and I'd ignore it. I needed to do it all … that worked for me - then.

These days, before I take any action, I listen – really listen - to that inner voice. I step back and wait until I hear it … and I try to understand it. Now, I'm in a better place.

You could call that voice just about anything that works for you: God, spirit, soul, spirit guide. It doesn't matter what anyone calls it … all that matters is that you learn to listen to it and trust that all will work out exactly as it needs to.

When you are ready to listen to yourself, try these **Simple Steps** to get clear on what you need to do … or not do:

- When there's a situation or a decision point in your life and you're uncertain about what to do, set aside fifteen or twenty minutes where you won't be disturbed.

- Take this time to clearly understand the situation and write down what you need to have an answer to. Revise the question until you are absolutely sure it's clear in your head. When it's crystal clear, read it out loud, or to yourself.

- Now, sit quietly and focus your thoughts on the question.

- Write down what comes to mind. Don't judge your thoughts. Keep writing until your thoughts on the subject stop.

- Read over what you have written. As you do, the resolution you are seeking will be clear to you.

Learning to trust the voice in your head may take some time. Start with something small and practice using these **Simple Steps**. As you gain experience in listening to your own voice, you will gain confidence. With confidence comes the ability to trust your own judgment every time!

Bless the Broken Road

I've had my share of challenges. Some have left big holes in my heart ... or royally messed with my head. If I think about some of them for too long, I might just crawl right back under the covers and never come out.

I was talking to a friend today, and she mentioned that she knew her life was broken. As I thought about what she said, it occurred to me that we're all broken at some point in our lives. We didn't come with operating instructions. We need to deal with whatever comes our way, learn from it and move on.

Some events are harder than others to move forward from. I can think of a few in my life. Every one of them though has taught me a lesson ... when I was open to learning from it. We all like to think we should have or could have been better, different, more assertive, less assertive, more giving, less taking ... those thoughts, however, keep us stuck in a place where we aren't happy.

Each of us is who we are because of our experiences (good and not so). That broken road is blessed and it leads us straight to our destiny.

If you're ready to honor your journey – potholes and all - try these **Simple Steps**:

- Acknowledge every piece of your life that you feel is broken. Examples may be: "I could have been a better wife/mother/friend" or "I made a very bad business decision."

- Next, decide what lesson you learned from the experience. "I learned I have to say what I'm feeling rather than holding it in" or "I learned I can't delegate the financial details of my investments."

- Reaffirm that you've learned a valuable lesson and forgive yourself.

Once you forgive yourself and convert mistakes into lessons, you free yourself up to be the person you are meant to be. And therein lies your destiny.

Focus on Past Successes

When it comes to our dreams, we tend to look to our past as an indicator of our potential success ... or failure. We judge ourselves and our chances for success by analyzing our history. That's really great if we have a track record of success ... and believe we can't fail. It's self defeating if we don't.

One of my last managers used to remind me of everything I'd failed at. There were so many successes ... but because of his "joking" negativity, I focused on what didn't work.

We've all heard the phrase "Learn from history or it will repeat itself." The problem is, if you focus on what hasn't worked for you, then you are likely to repeat it, or the experience will be similarly bad. It's classic Law of Attraction in action!

We're not our past, and it's time to realize that and stop the negativity that we may be hanging onto. Let's break the cycle that keeps us from our dreams.

I'm not going to say this is easy, but I believe if you take this **Simple Step** right now ... and continue to repeat it ... you'll change your future.

- Identify what you need in order to realize your dream. For example: if you want to start a business selling homemade cupcakes, you'll need a fabulous recipe, the funds to buy the ingredients, a place to bake them, a plan for selling them and the courage to get out and approach potential buyers.

- If your fear or angst is over actually pitching your product to others, go back in your past and look for times when you sold yourself. Perhaps you convinced your parents to let you go to a concert (you "sold" your responsible self). If you were hired by an employer, you successfully "sold" your skills to a manager.

- In each of these "sales," consider what you did to be successful. For example: you were prepared and well rested, you had researched the company, you had considered possible objections and had responses ready. Place your attention on those successful actions.

- Now, visualize your dream ... to have that wildly successful cupcake business. If you sold yourself to an employer for a job you needed ... can you imagine how great your sales ability will be for something you're so passionate about?

When you focus solely on your successes, you gain the strength, perseverance and commitment needed to realize your dreams. Focus on what you want ... and it's yours!

Be Real About You

Do you ever get the feeling that other people are happier than you are? Their marriages are happy, their jobs are great, their children are perfect and they are financially abundant. At least that's how it looks from the outside!

What happens when you encounter one of these folks and ask the perfunctory "How are you?" Do they respond with "Great!" causing you to respond the same way? You know it's not exactly accurate in your case ... why do you think it is in theirs?

When the truth never comes to the surface, things can feel pretty superficial. There's no real connection. And what's worse is, the person whose life you think is so charmed may be the one who needs a lifeline!

When you are honest and acknowledge your challenges, you give permission to others to open up and be more "real" with you.

This is one of those **Simple Steps** that's not easy, but it's time to stick your toe in the water:

- Start small ... if you open up the floodgates there's going to be a flood. The idea is to poke a hole in the dam.

- Take this approach with a personal friend - one you know well, respect and like.

- When asked how you are, respond with something along the lines of "I'm doing fairly well. I didn't receive the promotion I thought I would, so we won't be taking a vacation this year."

- Follow your admission with a positive statement: "I know I've got a couple of areas to work on that will make me more marketable/promotable, so I've started working with my mentor on ways to help me develop."

When you open up to another about your not-so-perfect life, you give them permission to do the same. In that space you relieve the pressure that you've been feeling. Then your friend has the opportunity to share their concerns too. And that feels better for both of you!

Passion Determines Persistence

How many times have you started a project and not finished it … whether it's a hobby or a new business venture? Do you end up seeing the fruits of your labor, or do you lose interest along the way? Does some kind of negative feedback cause you to abandon your efforts altogether?

Not finishing a project has nothing to do with failure. It does, however, have everything to do with passion.

When looking at a project, a job, a hobby … ask yourself if, deep inside you, this is something you really want to accomplish. If the answer is "no" or "maybe," walk away from it. If you get excited and start feeling that energy well up inside of you, then go full speed ahead! It's those endeavors that speak to your soul.

What are you giving yourself grief about not doing? Try this **Simple Step** to decide if you should let go or move forward:

- Take one project at a time - there's no need to address more than one. When you decide whether it's a go or not, then you can move to the next one. Don't pile things up on your plate.

- Write down or think through every part of the project until you have a comprehensive picture of it.

- Sit quietly and clear your mind of everything except the project.

- As you think about it, do you get excited? If not, take it off your plate. If you do get excited, and you feel this project is really important to you (not to anyone else), get moving! Take the time to write down all the details about the project and prioritize them. Start working through them in order, and check them off as you do.

When you decide that you're passionate about something, making a plan to accomplish it will keep you moving forward in the direction of your dream. It's when you have the passion that you persist!

Self-Respect

When you are trying to climb out of a bad place in your life, it's important to foster your own self-respect. Appreciating and valuing yourself means that there's less chance of backsliding. So how do you do that?

Remove this myth from your life: someone else's opinion matters more than your own. It does not!

How you feel about yourself relates directly to your happiness and your commitment to your goals. Feeling completely positive will guarantee your success. Think back to any point in your life when you felt the most in control and happy ... you were 100 percent responsible for those feelings.

Now wait ... let's suppress the "yeah, but" coming from you. If you've been searching for a job or a relationship for a long time, and you were passed by, it may feel like you aren't worthy. It's easy to get down when you feel rejected.

What have you learned from your attempts? Is the next "light bulb" in your life one more effort away?

Remember: making a consistent effort is the key. There's nothing about changing your life that is once and done ... there's no magic pill and certainly no way to delegate the task to someone else.

When you are ready, try one of these **Simple Steps** to launch yourself forward:

- Ask yourself: "Am I absolutely confident I've done everything I can to succeed?" This requires that you have a heart-to-heart conversation with yourself. Be honest. Attempting to fool yourself serves no purpose and only contributes to a lack of self respect. When you're sure you've made your best effort, your self respect will be solid. If you aren't sure you've done all you can do, then what's missing? Fill in the gaps.

- Quit second-guessing yourself. Rather than doubting yourself when something doesn't work out, look for the lesson to be learned from it. What do you know now that you didn't know before? How can you implement this new lesson in your approach?

- Wipe out the negativity in your self-talk. Replace "can't" with "can." Even if you can't physically do something yourself, use your creativity to find a way to accomplish the task. Work on changing your self-talk to self-respecting-talk.

You have everything you need to restore your life. Focus on respecting the person you are becoming. Then you will realize that all is as it should be - all is well!

Your Opinion of You

Are you struggling with being yourself in the face of pressure from your family or friends? Have your children decided they don't want you in their lives? Does your mother still believe she can tell you what to do and how to dress? Does your husband think his opinion matters more than yours?

If you answered "yes" to any of these questions, then try one of these **Simple Steps** to gain control over your own life without feeling guilty:

- Are you happy with yourself as a person? Are you fair, loving, supportive, a good friend, etc? If you believe you're a good person, then you're standing on a firm foundation. Build from there. If there's someone who wants to change you, thank them for caring. Gently let them know that you are happy just as you are and that you would appreciate their support.

- If you're not happy with yourself, determine what the key area is that you would like to change. For example, if you are easily brought to anger or tears, acknowledge where you are right now: "I get angry over insignificant issues and tend to blow up frequently."

    o Next, create an affirmation that supports your desired behavior as if it exists right now: "Small issues are not important to me. I take them in stride and focus on my happiness."

    o Carry your affirmation with you and refer to it often. Post it on your mirror, refrigerator or anywhere you will see it frequently.

    o Tell your family and friends you're making a concerted effort to change this part of your life and that you would like their support.

Whether you are the person you want to be or a work in progress, always remember you deserve to be happy! No one can take that away from you.

When you realize you have the ability to change your life to be what you want it to be, the only opinion to care about is yours.

Believe in Yourself

If we believe in our own abilities, we can achieve our dreams. So many of us know we're capable, yet we doubt ourselves. It's that doubt we need to wipe out of our memory banks.

Doubt isn't something that just showed up when we started examining our dreams. It's been dogging us for a long time. Every time we shy away from trying something new - socializing, speaking in front of people we don't know - that little (ok, not so little) aggravating thing called "doubt" creeps into our heads. We don't even get into gear because it's there nagging at us.

Some days we don't feel so confident. Other days we wonder if we're on the right track at all. And sometimes we desperately need someone else's approval. Our lives are works in progress. Believing we have more to gain than lose by moving forward closes the gap between where we are now and where we want to be. And that's progress!

To strengthen your belief in yourself, try a **Simple Step** or two:

- Take action! It's a great antidote to self-doubt. Do something you've been shying away from. It might be as simple as walking an extra block or calling up someone you would like to have as a mentor. It's totally up to you how bold you want to be. Once you take a step you'll have the confidence to try something else you've been avoiding.

- Understand the difference between "wanting" the support of others and "needing" their validation. As your confidence builds you may still ask for what you want from others, but you'll move forward in your decisions regardless.

- Believe this: you have more to gain by moving forward than you have to lose. Every attempt you make teaches you something, and that's progress!

When you believe in yourself and live from your heart ... you will continue to take steps that bring you closer to living your dream.

Break Through Your Roadblocks

Do you find yourself fretting over things – good or not so good? Just finding a way to worry about them? Do you worry about things you've done in the past ... even though the past is over?

I did. Some days my worrying sent me into a dark corner ... I wanted to pull the covers up over my head and never come out.

When I learned more about the Law of Attraction, I began to realize I was living a self-fulfilling prophecy. Whatever I focused on came to pass. When my focus was on financial concerns, I had plenty of them, and the worrying continued.

Now, I choose to focus on what's good in my life ... right now ... in the present. When I do that, I'm making the choice to be happy. Taking the next logical step, when I'm happy and focused on good things, more good comes my way.

All you need is a sliver of hope - a glimmer of light - to break through that wall of worry that surrounds you. Try these **Simple Steps** to add a little perspective:

- Identify what is causing you to worry non-stop. It isn't enough to just say, "I'm worried." You need to name what is causing your stress. Say it out loud or write it down, whichever you prefer.

- Since these are repeat worries, identify the worst thing that has ever happened.

- Now, step back and realize you've survived this before - even the worst - and you're still standing. If you haven't experienced what you would consider "the worst," then recognize that as much as you've worried about that happening ... it never has!

Regardless of what you are going through, if you look for the light, you will find it. Even if the light is a sliver from a crack ... it's a breakthrough!

Trust Your Instincts

Ever had a "hunch" about somebody or a certain situation? Ever gotten a strong vibe – good or bad? That gut feeling is our body talking to us, and often, we ignore it. Before you decide to take the advice of someone else, ask yourself a question: does this "feel" right? If you aren't sure ... wait. If it doesn't ... don't do it.

Just like any other animal on this planet, we're born with natural instincts, an alert system for our needs, our fears. That's how we survive. Trouble is, as we grow up we are taught to use our heads more, and our instincts take a back seat.

Our heads get filled with all sorts of stuff from other people – leaders, experts, gurus. They might know more than we do about certain things, but they don't know what is right for us. If you are listening to a "known" expert, and there is a knot in your stomach, RUN the other way.

Gut feelings are a powerful tool to propel us forward in our journey. They can help us do something bold: take a leap of faith, go against the grain or follow our passion and pursue our dreams.

Learning to trust yourself is a key step in achieving your dreams. You cannot delegate your happiness, your life and your future to anyone else's decision-making skills.

If you want to build confidence in yourself and trust your instincts, try these **Simple Steps**:

- Pick an issue where you need to make a decision. Start with something small at first. This is about building up your self-assurance.

- Sit quietly and consider your options.

- What is your first instinct? Follow it! When you start to second-guess yourself, you are going down the wrong path.

- Next decision … step up … work on something bigger.

When you start seeing the results of doing what feels "right," your confidence will soar. Trust your gut … you will never take the wrong path.

Take a Leap of Faith

I was chatting with an old friend tonight. Karen is one of the most positive people I know. She's outgoing, encouraging, supportive and smart as anyone I've ever known. Karen fell in love with Demola - a man from another country – someone she has never met in person. They video chat regularly and have developed a face-to-face relationship.

There was a time when I would have thought, "She's crazy to think about marrying a man she's never met!" Now, I believe that taking that "leap of faith" is not so crazy ... it's inspiring! What Karen is doing is listening to her soul ... she knows she's on the right course, for her.

We all have an internal guidance system that will steer us down the right path ... if we acknowledge it and are true to ourselves. In the most simplistic terms: if what you are doing brings you joy and makes you happy, you're on the right path. If, however, what you're doing stresses you out and makes you unhappy or in any way makes you feel bad, you're going against yourself.

Whether what you want to do is a giant leap of faith like Karen's or something a bit more mundane, your internal compass will always keep you on course.

Here are a couple of **Simple Steps** to help you recognize how your internal guidance system is working.

- On a notepad write down what decision you want to make. Be as clear as possible. Write it as if you were providing options to a friend. The idea is to clearly understand the decision you're facing.

- Next, write down your choices. Again provide sufficient detail so it's clear what options you have.

- Now, walk away from the decision for at least thirty minutes. Distract yourself with anything that will keep you from running over the decision.

- When you return, quickly look at each choice one at a time. Mark each choice with either a (+) or (-) beside it. This represents your immediate feeling upon reading the choice.

- Cross out all the (-). Rewrite the options (if there is more than one.) Repeat steps 2-4 until one option remains.

By clearing out the options that don't feel right, you'll be left with what does. And as the old adage says, "If it feels right, do it!"

Be Kind to Yourself

When times are tough, do you revert to a pattern of negativity: unhappiness, anger, depression, and blame?

All of us go through hardship and have daily frustrations and disappointments. When stressful events pile up, how do you treat yourself and others?

When you're out of your normal rhythm and being dragged down, remember to be kind to yourself. It's important to try one of these **Simple Steps**:

- Be aware of your thoughts and feelings. You don't have to suppress them, nor do you have to be carried away by them. Just hold them and be sympathetic to yourself. You've been through enough and you don't need to beat yourself up for being out of sync.

- Next, do something positive. Treat yourself to a massage, volunteer at a shelter or maybe go to an amusement park. Do anything that you associate with happiness - yours or someone else's.

- Lastly, plan your next few days. That will gently nudge you back into your routine and give you something to look forward to.

Take the time to channel your energy into a more positive place, and you will find yourself back on top of your game!

"Me" Time

Do you feel like all your energy has been zapped out of your body? Maybe you have a job that drains you, or maybe you're sick. Perhaps you've had a week of stress and drama.

When your energy is low, you feel your worst. There's so much you want to accomplish, and you can't ... then you feel even worse for being lazy. We usually beat ourselves up for needing down time.

Do you ever allow yourself any personal time? Let's not confuse personal time with making dinner, playing with the kids or doing the laundry!

"Me" time is when you close out the world and do what you want to do - for you. "Me" time is when you soak in a tub or sit down to read a good book. Perhaps it's going for a manicure or a facial. Or maybe it's taking a walk alone and enjoying the weather or the scenery. "Me" time doesn't have to cost you a cent.

Of course, you may have someone in your life that views your "me" time as cutting into "their" time. When that happens, you can say, "In order for me to be there for you, I have to be at my best ... and that means I need time to recharge my batteries."

Try out one of these **Simple Step**s when you need to grab some "Me" time:

- Before you start your day, set aside twenty minutes to sit in your favorite chair, enjoy your coffee and your surroundings. Maybe you have a window to look out with a beautiful view, or maybe you can sit out on a patio in the quiet morning. If you do this before the rest of your family gets up, you'll be ready for them.

- Rather than going out to lunch with coworkers, put on comfortable shoes and take a walk around your building or the block. You can even do this on a ten-minute break if you never seem to take lunch.

- Schedule a day of "me" time once a month. This works for those who can't take the time during any given day or week. Actually put the time on your calendar. Send the kids off to a friend, your spouse, out to play golf or to a ballgame. Then spend your day doing everything you want to do ... or nothing.

When you take time to restore your energy, you'll discover how much you actually have for other important people in your life.

Release It!

Let it Go

*Some people think it's holding on
that makes one strong.
Sometimes it's letting go...*

                            - Unknown

Release It! Let It Go
Introduction

Imagine what it would feel like to have the weight of the world fall off your shoulders. Picture it rolling off your back and falling like a heap at your feet. Step out and walk away from it. Feel the lightness of your body and your soul. Doesn't that feel great? It's a powerful visualization, and we'll talk more about that later. For now, let's get real about letting go of what weighs you down.

Whether it's something from your past, fear of the future or just the reality of your now, you have to be willing to release it. Turn it over to your Higher Power. Until you do, what is eating away at you will exhaust the energy you need to move forward in your life.

We can use the past to propel us forward, or we can allow ourselves to be stuck in another time. In either case, we give power to our experience. We can't go back in time and change the past. It's over. We can forgive ourselves or someone else, learn from the experience and use that hard-won education to make better decisions in the future. Every minute we live is an opportunity to learn something new that we can use along our journey.

For some, the fear of what might happen in the future is like standing in cement. The longer they stay in that place, the harder it becomes to break free. The truth is, we create fear in our minds and turn it into our reality. What we think about materializes, and then we feel justified in our fear. The really cool thing is if we visualize a positive future that will materialize too.

As you read this chapter, you might be experiencing something you're struggling with. What happens in our "now" is a result of prior thoughts and actions. In my case, I was constantly worried about money. I was sure that some catastrophic event would occur and I'd be penniless. Sure enough, I thought myself right into financial devastation. I could have stayed in that place by holding onto the same thoughts that brought me there, or I could change my beliefs and change my future. I chose to change my thoughts … and you can too!

We have to be willing to let go of the past, the fear of the future and our self-limiting thoughts in order to change our lives for the better. Once we realize what we are thinking and feeling (Know It! Tune Into You), then we can Let It Go and allow the baggage to fall to our feet. If you are ready to kick it to the curb and step into your future, then explore the **Simple Steps** that follow.

Are You in a Black Hole?

Did you know that black is a color that doesn't emit or reflect light? When you fall into a black hole you can't see the light of day. The color black, however, absorbs all the light that comes into it ... and that means that each of us has the potential to radiate light even in our darkest moments.

There comes a time when remaining in a black hole is worse than the reason you fell into it in the first place. If you've been in that place for any length of time, how do you crawl out? And as you are coming out, what do you do to keep from backsliding?

Does any of this sound like where you are ... where you've been ... or where you are trying to keep from going? If it does, you are not alone!

Google your situation and you will find hundreds - even thousands - of pages and people talking about it. Whether it's divorce, infidelity, death, job loss, foreclosure, bankruptcy, illness, challenges with children/parents/friends ... the sheer volume of information should be a graphic indicator that the path you're on is well traveled.

Before you can get out of the black hole, you need to know how deep it is. Try this **Simple Step** to determine where you are:

- Make a list of every single thing that's bothering you. Keep writing until you've committed all your worries to paper.

- Next, go back and read what you've written, one worry at a time. A couple things will happen:

  o When you see it in writing, you'll recognize it for what it is - nothing worth your time. Cross it off your list. (Notice that your worries just shrunk!)

  o You may also realize as you read it that your perception is harsh - even overly exaggerated. If that's the case, restate it more accurately. (It feels so much better to gain that perspective.)

o   Perhaps what you wrote is a clear depiction of your concern - good! (Understanding what is bothering you is the first step in fixing it.)

- Rewrite your list. Clean it up and get rid of the stuff that didn't matter or wasn't accurate.

- Read your revised list. Commit it to memory.

- Burn it! Shred it! Permanently destroy it! This step is symbolic ... but effective.

The act of eliminating your worries on paper is a first **Simple Step** to eliminating them from your life. Give it a try!

Remove the Past from the Future

There are times when we're haunted by past failures. Even though we say we're over them, some shred of that nightmare creeps into the "now." Before we know it, we're back in that place of negativity, reliving the pain.

When we look at the past to determine our future, we might repeat the experience. Sure, it may not be exactly the same, but it will be so close that it reinforces the negative image. The same is true for what we did well ... except that most of us forget our successes quicker than we do our shortcomings.

What if we choose to ignore the past? What if we choose not to "go back" and relive our perceived failures.

Would you be willing to set aside reliving your past in order to realize your dreams and experience how good life can be?

Try one of these **Simple Steps** when you are ready to banish your past:

- Just say "No!" When the negativity pops up, put it in its place. "No! I am not my past." "No! My life is not defined by my prior failures."

- Acknowledge the lessons learned. Every event in our life carries with it a lesson. Once you learn it ... you can move forward. For example: "I've learned that another person can't make me happy. I have to make my own happiness."

- Visualize your success! If you are truly sincere about pursuing your dream, then paint the picture of what success means for you. Add as many details as are important to you. The more real you see it, the more real you make it.

You are not your past experiences. You are, however, the result of the lessons ... the wisdom that you've gained from those experiences. When you look at it from that perspective, you can be grateful for even the most difficult challenges.

Be Done With It

How many times have you wanted something to just be over? A stress, a relationship, a disagreement, a phase. Sometimes it feels like negative events have a life of their own … they grow even though we want them to die a quick death. How can we move forward into the positive life we want in spite of events that seem to be keeping us down?

If you believe in the Law of Attraction, then you know that when we focus on what we don't want … we give it life. That's exactly the opposite of what we want to happen. So, our challenge is to think about what we do want. Easier said than done, right?!?

When you want to move forward from negativity, try one of these **Simple Steps** to drive the pink elephant out of the room:

- Purge - This can be a symbolic effort or a physical one … the choice is yours. Write down what is dragging you down. Then burn (safely), shred or throw the paper out with the garbage. If there are actual remnants, pack them up and take them to a shelter or other worthy charity. If they aren't usable, take them to the dump and throw them out of your life. Drive away.

- Defer - Oftentimes there are issues that need to be addressed at a later time. They hang over your head like taxes. Schedule what needs to be done at a future date. Write it on a calendar or on your computer. Set up a reminder and tell yourself you'll deal with it when it's appropriate. For now you are going to address more important issues … like being happy!

- Let Go - Turn it over to your Higher Power to handle. This is especially helpful when there is nothing you can do about it. Whether you pray, meditate or have a conversation with your Higher Power … say out loud, "I need you to take care of this." If something pops up that you've turned over to your Higher Power, just say, "That's my Higher Power's responsibility." Let it go.

Once this is done, focus on what you do want ... one **Simple Step** at a time!

Come Into the Light

You know the place ... the one where nothing seems to be going right and the light just isn't shining.

Are you in that place? Do you think you are on your way out when something sucks you back into the darkness?

Do you want to get out? That may sound crazy ... who would want to be where you are? But some people need drama in their lives. Others don't believe they deserve better. Then there are those who have been struggling for so long, they don't have the energy to get up and try again.

Unless you want to be in a better place, no person or **Simple Step** can help you. You have to want to help yourself.

Are you ready to let the light in? Try these **Simple Steps**:

- Be still. Let go of all the negative energy. Drain it out of your mind and visualize it flowing away from you. As it goes, picture sunlight surrounding you and warming your entire being.

- While you are in this more peaceful place, ask yourself what you know today that you didn't know before the lights went out.

- Now that you know something that you didn't know before, how will you live your life differently?

- Write down the first three things that come to mind and act on one immediately. When you have finished with the first one, move on to the next.

Even if you aren't in a dark place, you can use these **Simple Steps** to improve your life and happiness. The forward movement, the progress you make, will transform you into a person who is in control.

Face Fear

In the ever-changing world we live in, it's easy to get caught up in the events broadcast in the media. There's so much going on between the economy, political and religious conflicts, drugs, climate change … it's not surprising that we become fearful. Bad news sells advertising. Unfortunately, the almost singular focus on bad leads us to believe there is more ugliness than there really is. As with anything else … what we focus on we get more of.

If there is a situation or event that you worry about, then it's time to deal with it and come face to face with your fear. The way to do that is through examination.

When you dissect your fears, they lose their power and are ultimately diminished.

Try these to help eradicate your fear:

- First, name your fear. Articulate it. Use details. Let's use a fear of flying. You might be thinking: "What if maintenance isn't up to par?" "A terrorist might be on the plane!" "We could hit a flock of birds!" "Maybe the pilots are drinking!" "What if the plane misses the runway?" Write down anything that comes to mind.

- Next, examine the details. Using the flying example, Google "airline maintenance," "airline security," "birds hitting planes" (or vice versa), "pilot sobriety," "missed airline landings." Look at Wikipedia or the FAA website for results. Scan through them. These resources tend to give you a balanced approach to the issues. With each article you read, look at the issues around "frequency." For example, how many planes have crashed due to bird encounters in recent history?

- Once you make it through your research, you will have gained a much needed perspective … and you'll notice your fear has diminished.

Remember: you have the upper hand. Fears have no power unless you give it to them. Don't!

Let Go of the Ledge

Have you ever wanted to take a chance on something only to stay glued to where you are because you're afraid? I have. As long as I didn't have to move out of my comfort zone, I was "safe." But something was missing... and this little voice in the back of my head kept telling me I needed to change my life.

I began to think I needed to "let go of the ledge" - to spread my wings and fly, but somehow I just didn't know how to let go, or what would happen if I did.

Times when I did want to "go for it," I still had a "Plan B." You know what that is? It's what you are going to do when "Plan A" doesn't work.

I'm not saying there should never be a "Plan B" - some things just aren't in our control and could go a couple of ways, and being prepared for those options is a good thing. But for those actions that are in our control, constantly having a "Plan B" ready can mean our "Plan A" never has a chance.

There are a couple of **Simple Steps** to consider if you are ready to "let go of the ledge" and take a risk to bring about a better life:

- Make a list of everything in your life that you would change if you could. It doesn't matter if the change is small (drinking nonfat milk instead of 2 percent) or large (divorce). Next, organize your list so like items are together (drink nonfat milk, add fruit to my diet, plan dinners, walk). Decide which group is the most important for you to work on first. Pick the smallest change from that group and do it. Take a few days, or even a few weeks, to live with the new change. When you feel you have conquered that change ... pick another one from the same group. Repeat. While it might take you months, or even a year or more, to get through your list ... the changes you do make will stick.

- Identify the single most important change you want to make in your life. Reach out to your best friends and tell them about it. Ask for their support to help keep you accountable. Their role may be as simple as asking you what you do every day to work on your change or as involved as working on the change for themselves, too. Having a partner, someone who supports you and that you are accountable to, can be the difference between success or not.

When you are ready to stop hedging your bets and let go of the proverbial ledge, you'll find yourself taking a leap closer to your dream. Sure, it may be scary, but the rewards make it worthy for you!

Let Go of the Oars

As I was chatting with some of our friends recently, it was apparent that there are many people whose energy stores are zapped. Whether they are working in a bad environment, dealing daily with teenagers or unemployed and feeling they aren't carrying their weight – they're hitting their heads against the wall and ready to say, "Enough is enough!"

Do you ever feel that way?

I like the analogy Abraham Hicks uses for these situations. He calls it "paddling upstream." As long as you paddle against the current, you are not going to get anywhere. Sure, you can struggle valiantly against the current ... but in the end what have you accomplished? The struggle just wears you down.

If, instead, you let go of the oars and "go with the flow," you will go to where you need, and the journey will be much more enjoyable!

Tired of the struggle? Trying something different may bring relief in the form of a "break," and you might see the situation from a new perspective.

If your struggle is with another person, try this **Simple Step** to give yourself the relief you need:

- Clearly identify the issue. It's not enough to say, "My partner spends too much money." Instead get to the core issue. "My partner doesn't know how much money is in our account at any given time. He just likes to buy the newest things, and I have to be the gatekeeper. I don't like to be the bad guy all the time, but he doesn't give me a choice." Now, that's a clear statement of what is bothering you!

- Pick your time and communicate your concern to your partner. In the heat of arguments, your intent - and the message - has probably been lost. By being prepared for the conversation and having it when you are both calm, the message gets heard.

- Ask your partner for his ideas on how you can resolve the conflict. Determine what a good compromise is ... agree to it and write it down. Post it if you can and plan a follow-up each week - or as often as necessary - to keep the agreement fresh in your minds.

When you are both involved in determining a solution, then you both have buy-in ... and with that, the chances for success grow significantly.

If you are struggling against yourself, the **Simple Step** is:

- Identify and clearly articulate your challenge.

- List out the possible resolutions. Don't judge any of them and include anything from the obvious to ones that are really outside your comfort zone.

- Read over your list until you notice the one that you keep coming back to. Go with it!

Allow yourself to just float downstream (positive energy), and you'll realize how much better you feel. What was draining becomes energizing.

Let Go of the Past

There are events in our lives that leave an indelible impression. Some bring us to our knees, while others raise us up. The death of a child, a violent act or a tragic mistake are a few that come to mind. Even lesser events can be life altering.

In our most painful moments, we wish we could go back and make the changes that might have prevented these events from occurring. But we can't. We have to live in this moment and make the best of it.

Letting go of the past is tough. The only way to do it is to use what we've learned from these challenges to make our life ... and hopefully the lives of others ... better, now.

Try these **Simple Steps** when you are ready to move past your past:

- Take time to feel the pain. If you lost someone close to you, mourn and celebrate their life. Realize that while your time with them may have been too short, there are others who need you. Life is much too short. Be present for those in your life now.

- If your hurt arises from a relationship that isn't working/didn't work as you'd hoped, holding onto it keeps you in a state of pain. If you've been betrayed or hurt by someone else, realize that by allowing those feelings to dominate your life you're making a choice to permit that person's actions to continue to hurt you. The event is over. You are watching reruns. Turn the channel! How? As you start to feel the pain coming on, say out loud "NO! I'm not going to let this hurt me anymore. I am choosing to be happy." Repeat this ... even if it's multiple times in an hour. Doing so distracts you from the pain, and after a while you'll start saying "Yes" to happier thoughts.

- If you made bad choices, then acknowledge them. "I chose to invest in real estate, and it was the wrong choice for me." "I chose to drink/smoke/take drugs in the past." "I chose to quit school." Follow those statements with what you are choosing to do differently. "I have lost everything financially and know that going forward I will do my due diligence and not rely on gurus." "I abused my body by drinking/smoking/taking drugs, but I'm choosing to honor my body and my life by making better choices." "I may have quit school when I was younger, but I'm back now and I'm ready to learn!"

When we make the effort to release the pain of our past, we tell ourselves that it's time to start enjoying life again. This may take a little more time than we'd prefer ... however, when we are ready to let go of the past, we signal our willingness to live life to the fullest right now!

Starting Over

I used to think that starting over again somehow meant I had failed. Now I see starting over as an opportunity to do it "my way." Those first fifty-plus years were a steep learning curve. I made my share of mistakes, had a few regrets, made it past them and came to a place of peace. Starting over ... it's a blessing.

Did you find yourself out of a job after years in the same field, and you're wondering what you're going to do now? Did a relationship end, and now you find yourself single for the first time in many years? Perhaps your financial picture looks worse than it did when you first entered the workforce. As tough as all of these situations may be, when you look at them as a blessing, you'll discover that you have been liberated!

It's all about your perception. If you want to focus on everything that's bad, that's what you experience. Choose to focus on the possibilities ... they are endless. The key here is to keep your focus on what you want, not what you don't want.

When you're ready to shift your focus to one of freedom and opportunity, try one of the **Simple Steps**:

- Get out of the box you've been in and create your new calling. Now that you have a blank slate, decide what you want your life to be about. In my early days, I took the job that had the most potential, financial compensation and job security. I never took the time to decide what I "wanted" to do. Rather than rush back and take "any" job, take the time to decide what you want to do. Explore night classes, a total change in direction, volunteer with an organization that you'd like to work with.

- Write down all the things you've "lost." For example, if you're starting over again financially, your list might include: "I can't take vacations." "I can't afford a new car right now." "We have to cut back on eating out/movies." "We have to move out of our home and find a less expensive place to rent." Realize that all these changes are temporary. Right now you're choosing to regain your stability and build up an emergency fund. Take a good hard look at your list.

- Create a list of "needs" and "wants". Once you have provided for your "needs," plan to add something back in from your "wants" list - when it makes sense to do so. You now get to control your finances, rather than (a lack of) money controlling you.

- Mourn your loss, and then have a wake. Take some time to accept the fact that your life will never be the same. That doesn't mean you wallow in self-pity ... it means you pay homage to what was. Have a mock funeral or burn that life (figuratively) in a bonfire by the beach. Now celebrate your new life. The phoenix rises again and so will you, now that the chains of the past are gone. Have fun with this one ... laughter is good medicine too!

Starting over again may be a daunting task ... but when you see it as your liberation, you'll be celebrating. And that feels awesome!

Stop Worrying

I may not have an artistic bone in my body – I've always been the pragmatic one. But I do have an imagination - especially for "the sky is falling" scenarios.

Worrying about what "might happen" is a very bad use of a good imagination!

What snapped me out of my doomsday prophecies was a passage in a book that said 93 percent of the time what we worry about never materializes. So let me get this straight ... worry, fret and anxiety about what "might" happen has a 7 percent chance of coming to fruition? What a waste of time! Yes ... I quit worrying.

If you have faced work and financial insecurity, you may be using your imagination to drive yourself crazy. I know I have. My worries covered the gamut from being homeless to having to sell my car to make ends meet and everything in between. While none of this is anything to laugh about ... when you add in some perspective about the likelihood of your fears materializing ... you can relax and focus on taking action rather than being frozen with fear.

Try these **Simple Steps** to free yourself from worry:

- With a partner or close friend that you trust, take your concern and verbalize every bad thing that could happen. The more outrageous the better. When you actually say your concerns out loud, they lose their power. When you laugh at them, you gain your power.

- If you are always on the Internet, Google your worry. For example: "If I lose my job I will be homeless." You will be amazed at how much information is out there about your fear. There are solutions, blogs and articles that can help you. Knowledge is power. One word of caution here: if you come across a website that promises they can solve your problem for a fee ... RUN the other way.

- Breathe … focus on your breath as it flows in and out of your body. When you do this, you quiet your mind and take the focus off what you are worrying about. Try this for a few minutes. It may take some practice, but the more time you spend breathing, you give yourself the gift of clarity and perspective. When you have those, you can work though any problems that arise.

Imagine your life being worry-free. That kind of imagining will bring you peace.

Own It!

Take Responsibility

Accept responsibility for your life.
Know that it is you who will get you
where you want to go,
no one else.

— Les Brown

Own It! Take Responsibility

Introduction

Do you realize that you are 100 percent responsible for your life? You control your actions and your attitude. That's a simple fact, though it may not always be a popular one.

At a certain age, we move from our parents control to our own. Hopefully they were good teachers and we gained a strong foundation. From there we get to build our own lives, based on our own choices. We are responsible for the results of those choices, good and not so good.

If it all works out as we hoped it would, we can celebrate our success and take another step. When something doesn't work out, we own that result too. Failures are great opportunities to work even harder to find a better way next time. Every bit of knowledge we gain through making a decision and being accountable for the results propels us to another level of confidence.

If your inclination is to give up when things don't go your way ... remember, that's a choice too. You are responsible for quitting.

What about all the things that happen "to" us that we had no choice in: the illness, the natural disaster, our company going out of business, the economy? While you may not have any say in those events, you do get to choose how you react to them.

I've had my share of stuff happening "to" me. Between Jack being diagnosed with cancer and leukemia, my company being acquired and my position being eliminated, and my dad's sudden death leaving me as primary caregiver for my blind mom ... these events came as a shock to me, and it took some time for me to let them sink in. Once I got past the initial jolt, I was able to choose whether to deal with them or be buried by them.

It's in our attitude that we are able to turn adversity into triumph. We don't have to like what has happened. Everything in life happens for a reason, and

65

in time, the tragedy may become the event that propels us to our greatest achievement. It's all a matter of perspective. Yours.

When we look for the lesson in the failure and see the potential in every event, we are responsible for our happiness, our life and our dreams.

If you are ready to own your life, then try the **Simple Steps** in this chapter and take the reins!

Wake Up!

Are you drifting?

Not really sure what you did all day?

Worked all your life and now find yourself unemployed and realize you have nothing to hang your hat on?

At a loss because you realize your skill set doesn't transfer to today's job market?

Wondering why life passed you by and left you with nothing to show for it except maybe a few grey hairs and "laugh" lines?

WAKE UP! It's time to move forward!

Try one of these **Simple Steps** and check back into life:

- Plan Your Day. If you have always been one to take things as they come, then taking the time to create a "To Do" list will be huge! Write down everything you want to accomplish this week. Prioritize your list. This doesn't mean all the big projects are at the top (or the bottom). It means you have things listed at the top that you need to accomplish sooner, rather than later. On a calendar assign tasks, placing your higher priority items at the beginning of the week.

- Take a Class. It doesn't matter what you choose to take ... as long as it's something you want to learn.

- Choose a hobby or sport or anything that will be enjoyable. By committing to a scheduled event, you'll start planning the rest of your life around something that's fun for you.

- Reconnect. Make a list of friends you enjoy talking with. Choose two or three each week and call them. Use the time to catch up on each other's lives. If they live close, plan to meet for lunch or coffee. When you connect with others, you open up your life by talking about it, and that gives you the opportunity to move on.

Whether you think you've missed out on large events in your life ... or you feel like you're on autopilot and have no idea where you're going ... being actively engaged in your daily life will bring more joy to your waking moments!

Turn Off Automatic

Do you feel like your life is boring? You get up, go to work at a job you don't enjoy, come home, fix dinner, watch TV, go to bed and then do it all over again the next day. By the time the weekend comes around, you clean the house, do the laundry, shop for groceries and make up meals for the week.

When you have responsibilities, life takes on an "autopilot" quality that is safe. And there is comfort in the routine.

Do you want to move away from autopilot? Are you looking to find your voice or the next version of your life? Whether it's through a creative or more traditional outlet doesn't really matter as long as it's an expression of who you really are.

Try this **Simple Step** if you are in search of you:

- Make a list of all the things you have wanted to do (not things you want to have). Group them together by similar characteristics. For example: if four of your items involve travel, group them together.

- Now, take a look at your list. Which group has the most items listed? Take that group and make a list of steps you could take to work towards accomplishing those items. Using the travel example: you could go online and price your first trip or research where you are going. The goal here is to move you off the "couch" and down the path to your dreams.

If you are ready to live the life of your dreams, then it's time to stand up and find "you." The adventure of your lifetime starts your lifetime of adventure, and it all begins with your first step ... a **Simple Step**!

Shift Your Life Into Forward Gear

Are there times in your life when you feel stuck in neutral? Sure, there is plenty for you to do ... but instead of doing what you know needs done, you find little things to do. Those little things that create a sense of "doing something," however, are not important or even in the top one hundred of your "to do" list. Why do you spin your wheels rather than shifting into gear and moving forward?

Here are a few **Simple Steps** to help you move forward:

- Enlist the help of your partner, children or best friends. Whether you ask them to check on your progress or join you in your efforts, having a "partner" requires you to be accountable. Tell them what you are trying to accomplish and what you need them to do. For example: if your goal is to walk every day, tell your partner you're going to send an e-mail every day with how long or how far you walked. Even better, ask your partner to join you.

- Set up a rewards program for yourself. This doesn't have to be complicated. If you plan to walk every day during the week, reward yourself with a manicure when you do. If you keep it up for a month, make the reward bigger ... a facial or massage. If walking is your way to get back into shape, reward yourself with a new pair of jeans or other special piece of clothing that shows off your improved figure.

- Plan your downtime. This is a reverse of what you would expect to do when you have a long "to do" list. Pull out your calendar and mark off a day or two each week when it's your time to do what you love. That may be reading, going shopping or having lunch with a friend. What you do during your downtime should be what you enjoy most. As you check off items on your list, you are actually looking forward ... and when you look forward, you move forward.

As you shift into forward gear, it's important that you only glance back briefly. Acknowledge where you have been and move on. You can't change the past. Enjoy the journey that is waiting for you!

Cracking the Facade

How's your life going? Are you living your dream? Are you happy to get up and go to work? Do you enjoy your time with your spouse, your children, your friends? Do you feel like you're embracing life and it's all good? Or are you faking it?

Are you being honest, or have you developed the standard "I'm great" response when asked how you are? Do you believe your own story, or are you like millions of other people who don't want the world to know what's really going on?

When we put up a good front, we perpetuate the "Keep up with the Joneses" mentality. What if the Joneses are living the same lie? Okay, maybe that's a bit harsh ... maybe the Joneses don't want to let the world in on their challenges. We were raised to show no weakness.

What if, just for one moment, you broke through and created a crack in your façade ... if only with yourself? It's not about airing all your dirty laundry for everyone to see. But what if the next time you felt yourself going into denial you instead admitted that life wasn't going the way you wanted it to? Isn't it better to face the truth than try and fool yourself?

There's no crime in losing your job, getting divorced, filing for bankruptcy, discovering your child takes drugs or losing your home. They are challenges that millions of people face every year. While no one would wish these things on anyone ... they are not a reason to hide.

If you are facing a major challenge in your life, try this **Simple Step**:

- Every time a negative thought pops into your head, stop. Say "NO!" Out loud. (ok, you may want to say it to yourself if you aren't alone.) "NO!" Say it again. "NO!

- Next, state what you are refusing to entertain. "No! I am not a failure." "No! I am not a bad person because my husband left me."

- Next, turn your negative into something that makes you feel even a little bit better. "I've made mistakes, but I'm learning from them." "I am not a bad person. My husband made his choice, and now I'm making mine. I choose to move forward." "I have survived worse problems and come through them just fine. I'll do the same with this."

The goal here is to change your perspective. When you feel better about yourself, the challenge you're facing will be one you know you can overcome. Consistency is the key. Every single time you have a negative thought about your challenge, faithfully take this **Simple Step**.

Now, what would the world be like if all the "Joneses" took one **Simple Step** in their lives? Would the walls start tumbling down? And just like taking the Berlin Wall down ... the world would be a better place!

Dealing with Distractions

We get up each morning ready to take on a new day ... a plan in place ... and the phone rings. Before you know it, we've blown an hour. It's the latest emergency, and our plan evaporates. Ok, things happen. It's called "Life," and we just have to roll with it.

If we take the time to look at our distractions, we will see where all our time goes. But what do we do about getting it back?

Try one of these **Simple Steps** when you're ready to reclaim your time:

- Establish a new routine. Pick a time every day which is your time to focus. For example: if you send the kids off to school in the morning, take the first hour after they leave to work on your priorities. Let the rest of the family and your friends know that between nine and ten o'clock (or longer) you're going to be tied up daily (or on a particular day). Now, stick to your routine and turn down any request to schedule something during your time. In a short time this will not only be your habit, but it will also be common knowledge that you are not available.

- Create a quiet space in your home. When you need to focus, go there and leave the cell phone and computer elsewhere. You may need to train your family to leave you alone (except in case of an emergency). A good way to do this is to explain to them what you want to accomplish and ask for their support.

- If your work is on the computer, turn off all "notifications" - bells, e-mail, instant messengers or any other programs that signal you of an event.

When you make your priorities a priority, you'll discover a little more time in your day. And those extra minutes - or hours - may be just what you need to reach your goals!

Be Your Own Best Friend

Are you your own worst enemy? I know I've been mine.

I learned very early in life that everyone else's needs took priority over my own. I became really good at handling their responsibilities and duties. Being selfish was considered a weakness. I never quit when it came to the needs of others, but as an adult I became really good at quitting ... especially anything related to me personally (exercise, diet, etc.).

Are you doing anything that's undermining your happiness? This is the time for self-examination (not to be confused with self-loathing).

Try this **Simple Step** to increase the odds that you will succeed this time:

- Decide on a goal and make it your top priority.

- Write down everything you have tried in the past in order to accomplish your goal.

- Beside the effort, note what you did to undermine yourself.

- Next, write down what you will do differently this time.

- Take all your "instead" efforts and make a list. Post it where you'll see it several times a day - refrigerator, mirror, car dashboard, computer.

Make this year the one that tips the scales in your favor. Be your own best friend. Know that your life will be so much happier when you do!

Regaining Control

Everything in life has a cycle. Relationships, jobs, raising children - even how we deal with change can take on an almost predictable pattern. Life itself is a cycle. Sometimes we're flying high; other times we're not. It's those times when we're at the bottom, when we just can't catch a break, that we need to take action in order to break the pattern and create a new, more positive path.

When you're trying to break the cycle, there are two really important **Simple Steps** to consider:

- First: Acknowledge what is really going on in your life. This is not the time to stick your head in the sand or listen to someone tell you that the world is rosy. Until we come to terms with what we're dealing with, we can't really deal with it. Make a list, write it down, document what is on your shoulders right now. Own it. Once you allow yourself to acknowledge your stresses, you can go about working on them.

- Second: Prioritize. We tend to think the whole world is caving in on us when it's really only one or two problems. Our perspective gets jaded from stress, and we tend to see everything as black. It's not. Identify what really needs your attention and then recheck everything else on your list. Remind yourself that these other things aren't really a big deal and can wait. Or ... they aren't anything, and you can just forget about them or turn them over to your Higher Power to deal with. Focus only on what you have to!

Life throws us all sorts of curves, and sometimes the wild pitches hit us in the head. The question becomes: is it a wake-up call to make a change? Only we can decide for ourselves. And that decision is where we regain control!

Deal With It

Sometimes we smile because we don't want anyone to know we're in pain. Eventually we realize that what lies beneath the painted-on face isn't going away.

Unless we deal with what's bothering us, we can't move forward with our life ... let alone our dreams. And the truth be known ... the brave face is really transparent.

When you're ready to move beyond your pain, try one of these **Simple Steps**:

- Seek professional help. If you've been dealing with the issues for a long time, a counselor, therapist, coach or minister may provide you with some insight that makes all the difference.

- Talk to your partner, spouse, respected friend or other trusted person. Tell them what is bothering you and ask for their help and support. While it doesn't mean they take on your challenges, sharing them lessens the burden.

- Volunteer at a homeless or women's shelter, food bank or other charity that helps those in need. In doing so, you will gain a new perspective. Helping someone else ends up helping you.

- Spend time each day visualizing what your life will be like when this problem is resolved. Don't focus on how this is going to happen ... go directly to living life as you dream it to be. When you visualize, you see yourself happy and enjoying life as you choose it to be. Put as much emotion and excitement into feeling great. Do this for a few minutes every morning or night, and you will set the resolution in motion.

Challenges are part of life. Once you deal with them, rather than hide from them, you can move beyond your pain, and that smile on your face will be a real one!

Push the Limits

We all have our comfort zone. It's easy there. We don't have to stick out our necks ... we risk nothing. We may be really good at what we do, so we keep on doing it because in that space we are content and oftentimes appreciated.

When, however, we push ourselves outside our usual limits, we experience growth. Sure, it may be scary ... but the rewards make us realize we have no limits beyond what is in our heads.

If you have reached your limit with the "as is" of your life, then try these **Simple Steps** to push beyond your comfort zone:

- Enroll in an adult or continuing education class that interests you. Pick something that has always fascinated you. It may be here that you find your next "calling."

- Volunteer to work with seniors, children or animals. This enables you to use your experience, yet see life from a different perspective.

- Pick something in your life that you always do but wish you didn't. It may be a request from a friend or family member (babysitting, loaning money, running errands, etc.). Then do the exact opposite of what you would normally do. Say "Yes" instead of "No" or vice versa. Then stand your ground. This doesn't mean you are being unkind. It means you are doing what you want to do for a change. At first you may feel a bit guilty ... but when you realize it's ok ... you're going to feel so much better!

When we push outside the boundaries of our self-imposed limits, we discover a whole new part of ourselves. We realize our strength, we enjoy new experiences, and most of all, it gives us the courage to expand our reach again in the future.

Find the Lesson

Maybe you've heard the phrase "What doesn't kill you makes you stronger." I, for one, don't believe that everything in life has to be a struggle in order for me to be strong.

What I do believe is this: there's something I'm supposed to learn from every "challenge" that comes my way. Whether it's losing my job or failing to recognize a scam artist ... there is always something good that comes out of it. I just have to be open to seeing it.

There are times when stuff happens (I'm being nice here), and I want to give someone a piece of my mind. Of course, if I had done that every time something didn't go my way ... I'd have no mind left to give anyone a piece of!

At the end of the nightmare, I always realize there was a lesson for me. When I lost my job, the lesson was that being loyal to a company that isn't loyal to its employees was a mistake. From the real estate scam, I learned that everything that involves my financial security requires more of my time.

Now that I've had time to sit back and think about the challenges in my life, I realize I could have learned my lessons sooner if I had been open during the crisis. Instead, in the heat of the moment, I couldn't see past my own anger. And that served no purpose.

What are you not seeing past? If you're experiencing a challenge of your own right now, try this **Simple Step** and see if you can glean the lesson sooner:

- Spend five to ten minutes writing down exactly what you are going through. Be factual about the details. Leave the emotions out of it.

- Identify the parts of your challenge that are the most worrisome for you. Write those down.

- Next, for each of your concerns, write down all the possible outcomes. These should cover the range from nothing will come of it to the sky is falling.

- Read through your list of options. Cross out all the ones that seem to be highly unlikely.

- What remains on your list are the things you need to focus on. This clarity enables you to take the emotion out of the crisis and provides much needed perspective. What had seemed like your worst nightmare is now just another opportunity to learn.

As you get better at looking for the lessons in the middle of a crisis, you'll realize that nothing is a crisis. And there is peace in that place.

When Others Challenge Your Happiness

There are people who come into our lives, perhaps even relatives, who seem to send us running in the opposite direction. They don't understand us ... or we don't understand them. At times we may wonder if their actions are intended to hurt us

It's when others are unkind, or their actions don't make sense to us, that we need to be the most understanding. No two people were raised the same ... even if they are from the same family.

Do you have someone in your life who's hostile or ignores you? If so, try one of these **Simple Steps** to change how you deal with them:

- Bless them. Whether in person or silently, make the effort to wish them happiness. When they are mean or unkind, they are usually coming from a place of pain. Nothing you can do will change that. If you wish them happiness, you are sending out positive energy. It may be the only positive energy they have realized. One note: if you wish them well in person, be sincere. Don't fall into their negativity

- Leave them alone. This may not be an easy step ... especially if it is someone you love. Absence does make the heart grow fonder ... if it is meant to be. If it isn't, the distance will help you move forward in your life. Remember, you can't make someone love you. You can love yourself, and you can choose not to base your self-worth on another person's opinion.

- Walk away. If someone seems determined to be unkind or mean, don't stand there and take it. Even if they are coming from a place of pain doesn't mean you have to be injured. If they follow you, keep walking, get into your car and drive away if you have to. If you need to say something, let them know you'll be there to talk to them when they are in a better place. One note here: if you are dealing with someone who tends to be violent or abusive, seek professional assistance. Most situations aren't this dire; however, only you can make that determination.

Life is meant to be happy, but sometimes people aren't. That's their choice. Make your own happiness, and realize you can't change them. You can live by example and focus on your own happiness.

Managing Stress

At the end of the day, are you able to lay your head down on the pillow and fall asleep? Do you feel you've done well? Have you been kind? Have you done an honest day's work? Have you helped a friend?

I have thoughts that keep me up at night ... and each one relates to something I should or should not have done. It's those nights, though, when I realize I'm happier when I do for others.

When you're dealing with stress in your life, and it's keeping you up at night, it's even more difficult to manage it ... let alone recover from it.

One of the best ways of managing stress is to change your focus ... and one of the best ways to change your focus is to do for others. As difficult as your life might seem, there's always someone who can use your help. When you turn your attention to helping someone else, you manage to forget about your troubles for awhile. Even more importantly, it gives you a much needed break. And in the space between your stress and helping others, you gain a new perspective. That break may just be what you need to be able to sleep at night.

If you are ready to change your focus, try these **Simple Steps**:

- Take your children and visit a local nursing home. Even if you don't know anyone there, sit and talk to the residents – it's a nice surprise for them.

- Bake cookies and deliver them to your local fire department or hospital.

- Gather up clothing and linens to donate to a local shelter. Deliver them yourself and inquire if there is anything else you can help them with.

When you manage your stress by turning your focus on helping others ... they, of course, benefit ... but so will you. With a clear head you can sleep at night. And after a good night's sleep, you are better prepared to deal with what you need ... for you.

Have You Played Today?

Have you played today? Did you color with your children, enjoy a game of tennis or perhaps sit around with friends and have a good laugh? What have you done in the last week, the last month or even the last year that was fun? Maybe you can't remember the last time you "lightened up" or "let go."

If all you you've been doing is working and being the responsible one, then it's time to take time for you and have some fun! Besides relieving stress, playing allows you to gain perspective. Not everything in life is serious.

When you are ready, try one of these **Simple Steps** to lighten up:

- Schedule time in your day for fun. For those of you who are planners, this is right up your alley. Now, use the time you've scheduled to laugh. Stock up on old "I Love Lucy" reruns or your favorite comedy shows. Even if you only have ten minutes, you are sure to get a laugh in!

- Take a walk. Along the way try skipping. Remember how you used to love skipping as a child? You are never too old to have a bounce in your step. If you feel awkward, then feel free to laugh at yourself.

- Do the opposite of what you usually do. If you have a routine at home, do it in reverse if you can or do something totally different. Enjoy the small variety this brings to your life and notice the perspective shift. When you fumble with something new, laugh it off … look for the humor in your predictability.

Each moment of the day we get to choose whether to enjoy our journey or feel the drudgery. When you decide to have fun, I promise you'll make more room for play in your life.

Choose It!

You Have Choices

Everything is something you decide to do, and there is nothing that you have to do.

– Denis Waitley

Choose It! You Have Choices

Introduction

Think quick ... burgers, chicken or tofu? Smile or frown? Go to bed or stay up? Let go or hold on? Believe or doubt? In a matter of seconds we make choices that rule our day and determine our destiny. Or not ... It's our choice.

Every single thing that happens in our life involves a choice. If someone else makes a decision without us, we still get to choose how we'll deal with it. If something happens to us, we get to decide how we'll react to it ... or not. Even when we think we had no choice at all, we get to choose our attitude towards it.

The absolute beauty of this life is our ability to live by choice. No one can make us unhappy if we don't choose to be. And we can choose to be happy even in the worst of circumstances. No one can force us to believe one way or another ... it's our choice. We get to decide if what they say works for us or not.

As we work with choices in this chapter, there are two key points to keep in mind.

First, no decision is permanent. We make choices based on the best possible information we have at the time. When circumstances change, we are free to make a new choice. If you find yourself regretting a decision, refer to "Release It!" and turn it into a lesson that makes you better prepared for the next part of your journey.

Second, your attitude makes all the difference. When Jack was diagnosed with cancer, it would have been easy for him to be depressed and to worry. Instead, he decided that 99 percent of his body was still healthy, so he chose to focus on that 99 percent, not on the 1 percent that wasn't. His attitude made all the difference as he dealt with the surgery and radiation.

Even in the worst of circumstances — your spouse leaves, your job is eliminated, you are faced with grave illness or injury - you have the ability to choose how these events impact your life. You get to choose how to make the best of your life ... because it is yours to live.

As you explore this chapter, remember that everything - even your choices - happen for a reason. Give yourself the freedom to explore your options, and then ... take the **Simple Step** that speaks to you!

Create Your Own Reality

When you were growing up, were you taught to be practical? Go to school, get a job, stay loyal to the company, get married, have children ... do what a good husband/wife is supposed to do.

We are all on this journey of life, and no two paths are identical. When someone tells you to "be practical," they are making an attempt to define your life by their standards. The same is true for anyone who tells you to "get real." It's up to you to define your own reality according to what is important to you.

Everyone has responsibilities. I'm not suggesting you neglect legitimate responsibilities to find what makes you happy. Instead, adapt your responsibilities to include creating the life of your dreams. For example: if you're not in a satisfying job but you need to pay the bills, start looking for a new job while you're still employed. If you're in an unhappy relationship and have children to consider, decide what environment is best for their development and create it. Remember: every decision is one you freely make.

Try one of these **Simple Steps** when you are ready to choose your own reality:

- Make a list of factors or experiences you know would contribute to your happiness.

- Prioritize your list ... then start working on your top item.

- Communicate to those around you what you're doing and why it's important to you. Ask for their support. Be grateful if you receive it ... be determined to persevere if you don't.

Others may not like what you're doing, but you can't make them happy any more than they can make you happy. Live the life you choose! Create your own reality! It will feel so right, you'll wonder why you waited so long!

Choose to Be Happy

How's your day going? Did you start off on a high note and you're having fun? Or are you dragging and not really thrilled about the way things are going?

If you're flying high, looking forward to your day and feeling happy to be alive ... wouldn't it be great if you could replicate those feelings on days when you're not quite there?

Right now, at this very moment, you alone have the power to turn your day into what you want it to be! Circumstances don't determine if your day is good or bad ... your attitude does.

You may have heard this quote by Viktor Frankl: "The last of human freedoms – is the ability to choose one's attitude in a given set of circumstances." Frankl, a holocaust survivor, lost most of his family in the concentration camps. Because of his attitude, he not only endured but helped others to survive as well.

While most of us will never experience the degree of pain and suffering that Frankl endured, we too can choose how we deal with our life's circumstances.

We all have the choice to be happy or not. How you focus your energy will generate more of the same. It's the basis of the Law of Attraction. Which do you prefer: to draw more good things into your life or keep the bad coming your way? It's a "no brainer" for me ... what about you?

Try these **Simple Steps** to bring more happiness into your life:

- Breathe. Breathing is something we do unconsciously. However, consciously focusing on breathing in and out is calming. Close the door, go to a park or any place you won't be disturbed. Take five minutes and do nothing ... just breathe in and breathe out. Don't worry about changing the way you breathe ... just pay attention to it.

If your mind wonders, acknowledge the thought and then refocus on your breath.

- Walk. Get out of the house or office. Even if it's only for five or ten minutes. Walking helps you deal with your thoughts without distractions. When you have time to think … you can think things through. When your mind is clear … you can consider your options. And when you realize you have options … you're back in control.

- Volunteer. When you give your time to help others, you feel better. You gain perspective. Whether it's making a meal for a sick friend or helping out at a charitable organization, the act of giving does wonders for your attitude!

Each of these **Simple Steps** requires little of you, but the rewards are great. Make a decision to be happy … and watch your happiness grow.

When People Disappoint You

Throughout our journey, we're going to encounter plenty of people who let us down. It's frustrating, but true. We're all human ... we're disappointing them as well.

It's been said that if you don't expect anything from anyone, they can't disappoint you. That's one way to deal with it. But that would mean closing down ... and cutting yourself off from the good stuff in life as well.

If we learn to accept disappointment as part of life and figure out a way to deal with it, we can still be open to joy and happiness – nothing else really matters.

Here are a couple of **Simple Steps** that will help you deal with the disappointment, while maintaining your sense of self:

- Take a "Time Out." It will be natural to feel every range of emotion from sadness to anger ... and a few you may not want to admit to. What's important is that you realize you're going through a grieving process. Give yourself the time to feel every one of the emotions that come to you. Don't, however, act on them. This would be a good time to experiment with keeping a journal. When you write out what you feel, you help to release it

- Next, clearly identify how this disappointment impacts you and your life. If you are in harm's way, then, of course, it's time to walk away. If it's just your feelings and your pride that's hurt, move onto the next Step.

- Don't take it personally. People do things for their own reasons ... reasons that probably have nothing to do with you. Work on changing your perception of the situation and don't let the disappointment be an excuse to hold onto misery. Let it go.

In the end, only you can decide how this issue defines you. The choice is 100 percent yours. Choose to be happy!

Shift Your Perspective

When I lived in Texas, I would often watch the sunset from our back patio. We had a terrific view ... and they were awesome! My mom lived in the house behind us, and one night I moved over to her patio when the sun was going down. I could see the beautiful colors of the sunset ... but it was different than the view from my patio. What I saw was a gorgeous reflection of the sky in her pond. Amazing what moving just a few feet does for the view!

The same is true in life. When you look at the same thing from the same vantage point, you can see only one view. Tweak your perspective just a fraction and an entire new world opens up for you.

It's our choice to change our perspective. We don't have to have a detailed plan ... we can simply get off our patio and take a **Simple Step** over to the patio next door – so to speak! Voila! Different view!

While the change is simple, that doesn't necessarily mean it's easy. If you've believed one way for years, you can't flip a switch and suddenly believe the exact opposite. What you can do, however, is consistently practice the change in perspective. Repetition is a good thing here!

Are you ready? Try these **Simple Steps** when you sincerely want to change your perspective:

- Choose a belief that isn't serving you well. For example: I believe I'll never lose weight.

- Clearly state or write down what you believe right now: "I've tried all the diets, and while they work for awhile, I never stick with them."

- Next, write down what you want to believe: "I'm losing weight at a slow and steady pace. I make reasonable food choices and walk daily."

- Act "as if." Fill your pantry with good, healthy options. Place your walking shoes by the door as a reminder to walk

- Repeat and act "as if" you are successful!

As you progress, slow and steady, towards your goal and consistently act "as if" ... guess what? Your new perspective becomes your only perspective!

Your Past: When Others Won't Let You Forget About It

Have you made changes in your life and you want others to believe that? You've moved on, but your friends still see you the way you were, and their perception of you won't budge.

People like to remind us of our past. That's how they saw us. That's how they defined us. And they got used to us being that way. Maybe our past made a good story, and they were used to repeating it. If we had a particularly colorful past or made some mistakes, there are those who want to remind us of that ... or worse ... they want to hold it over our heads.

Change is scary for them, too! Even if it's only their perception of you that has to change.

What do you do when others want to keep you down even though you've stepped up to the plate? Here are a range of **Simple Steps** to try, depending on the significance of the change:

- Ignore them. If that doesn't work ...

- Have an open, honest conversation. This works when it's someone close to you such as a family member or good friend. Tell them that making this positive change is important to you, and that you need their support. Let them know their comments aren't helping. If they don't believe you, then ask them to give you a chance to show how you've changed. In order to do that, they need to keep their opinions to themselves. People close to you should want to see you succeed. If they don't, try the next **Simple Step**.

- Sometimes friends and family can feel insecure when you make a change. Perhaps they feel they'll be left behind, or worse, that you are better than they are because you have changed. When your open, honest conversation doesn't seem to be working, ask them directly why they are being unsupportive of you. Dig deep to get to the heart of what their real issue is. They may or may not tell you. If they do, assure them that you love them, and that just because you've changed doesn't mean your feelings about them have. If you can't get to the heart of their concerns, let them know you understand, but as long as they feel that way, they're choosing to live in the past. You are not.

- Perhaps your situation involves your work. Mine did. Sometimes those are the toughest to get through. What you say and what you do can be very different. Your boss, peers and other coworkers need to see sustained change before they are going to believe you. Only you can decide if you can ride it out until they do. If you are worn down by their negativity, start looking for other employment options. A different department, company or even another line of work may be called for. In my case, leaving my company was the best thing that happened to me. It gave me the clean slate I needed to be the person I chose to be.

Changing who you are as a person to the person you want to be is a liberating experience. But it's not easy when others want to keep you locked in the past. Just remember: it's up to you to live in the now. It takes perseverance, but in the end ... you will never regret being your authentic self.

Same Old Problem ... New Approach

Have you ever wondered when the struggle is going to end? You argue with those close to you, and you realize the whole discussion is a broken record. If you've had that argument dozens of times before ... and nothing changes ... when do you stop hitting your head against the wall?

At what point do you realize that you're spending so much time at odds that it's overshadowing your love for one another? Do you miss your happier life?

If you are at a point in your relationship where you want the adversity to end, then perhaps it's time to try something radical.

We can only change ourselves. We can't *make* anyone else do what we want them to do. Sure, there may be some cases of leverage, but does that result in you being respected in these long-term issues?

If you are tired of the stress, try one of these **Simple Steps** to move into a better place:

- Stop arguing. (I didn't say this one was easy - just simple.) When the subject arises that precipitates an argument, say something like this: "You and I need to agree to disagree on this. I respect your position and ask that you respect mine." Then walk away. Repeat as often as necessary until the other person realizes they aren't going to get anywhere with you.

- As the argument starts to surface and tensions build, say, "You are an important part of my life, and I don't want to argue with you. How can we compromise?" Then let them come up with a suggestion. Be willing to negotiate options and give your commitment to use the solution agreed upon. Ideally, you would write down the solution and sign it (but that may be pushing it a bit the first time).

- Do the exact opposite of what you have done all along. For example, if you insist that you be the one to drive when you go to the store, hand the keys over. If you are the one that writes the checks or pays the bills every month, set up a time to do it together. Do you only want to go to certain types of movies? Agree to alternate who chooses the movie. When you introduce a new approach to an old problem, give it a chance to work. After all it has been many years and arguments in the making ... you can't expect the resolution to be once and done.

As you start to see the results from your new approach, don't forget to acknowledge them. That positive reinforcement and thanks goes a long way to a better relationship and a happier life.

Overwhelmed

We have so many responsibilities on our plate, it's hard to know how to get it all done. And the worst part is ... we believe we have to do it all!

Have you ever felt this way? If so, you're not alone. There are thousands of stories from people just like you who have too many balls in the air. Even if you're a juggler ... you can't sustain that act for long!

Too much on your plate? Too many balls in the air? Here's a **Simple Step** to help you:

- Organize and prioritize. Make a list with everything you think needs to be accomplished. Mark a "1" by your top priorities. (Realistic top priorities. Doing your teenager's laundry isn't one of them!) Place a "2" by things you know you have to do, eventually. Then mark a "3" by anything someone else has asked you to do or those things that aren't time sensitive.

- Next take all of your "1" items and decide what comes first, second and third. If you have more than three items, move the others to the "2" category. Now, take your "3's" and write them on a separate piece of paper with this heading: "The Responsibility of the Universe." These are all the things you are not going to make any effort to do. If they need done to be done, delegate and let someone else deal with them. When you finish doing your "1" items, you can move a "2" up in line. The rest of the "2's" are on hold.

Realize that you don't have to do it all. When you focus on what's important and eliminate what isn't, you'll never drop a ball again.

Focus Your Energy

Have you heard the phrase "Life gets in the way"? It's usually spoken when good intentions get sidetracked for long periods of time.

Our "to do" lists and responsibilities seem to grow longer every day. The things we want to do get buried under everything we think we have to do.

When our heart's desire is at the bottom of that pile, it's time to take a good hard look at our priorities and start focusing our attention on what's important in our lives ... being happy.

Try these **Simple Steps** to focus your energy on your dreams:

- Embrace "No." Don't take on every request you receive. While you may have to drive your ten-year-old to the doctor, you don't have to bake brownies every time you're asked.

- Delegate more. Delegate "learning opportunities" to your children or spouse (coworkers too). Alternate nights of responsibilities, assign chores, list all the tasks and ask everyone to choose which jobs they will take on.

- Once you remove responsibilities from your plate, schedule your new "free" time for pursuing your dreams. Make a commitment to yourself and be passionate about your choice.

When you channel your energy towards your dreams, you'll see miraculous progress quickly ... and that feels good!

Choose to Forgive Yourself

We've all made our share of mistakes. We've made decisions that put our families through the ringer and screwed up relationships ... the list could go on and on.

I can't go back and change my past ... but I can learn from it, and I have. The consequences of my actions are my responsibility. By experiencing these darkest hours I learned valuable lessons that weren't part of my formal education. And in the end, the lessons made me the person I am today ... and that's progress!

I am not proud of all the things I have done in my past; but I am not ashamed of them either. Every choice I have made in my life (whether good or not so good) has brought me to this very place.

- Michael Merritt

If you are struggling and can't seem to forgive yourself, try one of these **Simple Steps** to move forward in your life:

- Clear the Air. If you've done something to hurt or alienate someone, apologize. Whether you write a letter, e-mail, call or meet them face-to-face ... be the bigger person. Make the effort to acknowledge that your actions hurt them and it wasn't your intent to do so. You don't have to make excuses or try to justify your actions. Keep it simple. Once you apologize, it's up to them to accept it or not. You, however, have taken the first step and you can move forward.

  A couple of notes about this **Simple Step**: if the other person does not accept your apology, that's their choice. They may even choose to move forward without you in their life. Each person has to do what is best for them.

- Take Personal Responsibility for Your Actions. Regardless of whether another person is involved or not, recognize and accept your culpability. When you admit to yourself and, perhaps, others your role, you control your next steps. If you choose to blame others, then you believe you have no control over your life and that you're a victim. Are you? Probably not ... or you wouldn't be looking to forgive yourself.

- Step Back. We are often so deep in our regrets and the emotion of the situation that we lose our objectivity. If your best friend had done what you regret, what would you say? Is she overreacting, making a mountain out of a molehill, can't let it go? Coach yourself as if you are your own best friend and take this advice to heart.

- Look for the Lesson. There's a lesson to be learned in every one of life's challenges. Until you realize what the lesson is, you can't move forward, and you might repeat the same mistake. Try this: sit quietly where you won't be disturbed and ask yourself what you would do differently if you could go back in time. Acknowledge that you can't change your history; however, you know more now than you did when you made your original decision. Now, give thanks for the lesson. Once you realize that you are wiser, forgiveness follows.

It's your choice whether to forgive yourself and move forward in life ... or not. Forgiveness releases you to live the life of your dreams. Without it you remain stuck in the past ... and that feels bad. Choose forgiveness because in doing so you are choosing to be happy - and that feels good!

When You Feel Sad and Alone

There are times in our lives when we feel sad and alone. Holidays can be particularly hard, especially after the death of a loved one or when the kids are with their spouse's family. If you've lost your job and your support system, the isolation can be extremely difficult. Or perhaps you've become a single parent or empty nester, and you're alone more than not. It's important to understand what you are feeling. It is real.

If you find yourself in that place between the blues and the black hole, know that being there is a choice. Your feelings may be natural, but that doesn't mean you have to let them run wild and take over. When you realize that your attitude is a choice, then you can decide to choose a more positive one.

Here are some **Simple Steps** to help refocus your thoughts:

- Take at least ten minutes to yourself with absolutely no one around. Out loud, say exactly how you are feeling: "I'm sad because by best friend died, and I feel responsible." "I'm afraid to be alone." "What would I do if something happened to my husband?" Elaborate on every worry or bad feeling you have. When you have it all out, take a deep breath. Sit calmly and turn your worries over to your Higher Power to deal with. This exercise transfers your stress to a power greater than your own. Then it's all about trust, faith and knowing.

- If you find yourself physically alone without family or pets to share your holidays, go out and help others. There is always someone who is in a more difficult place. Volunteer to help serve dinner at a shelter. Bake cookies or dessert and take them to a center for women and children. Go to a local hospital and rock babies or visit patients … share your kindness.

- If your friends and family live far away, download the "Skype" application on your computer. You will need a web cam, and you can pick one up inexpensively at a Best Buy or Radio Shack. Skype allows you to see each other as you talk. It's a great way to make a closer connection.

When life isn't the way you want it to be ... change it. Surround yourself with positive people and share your positivity ... the choice is yours. Sure, it may not be the easiest thing to do, but it will feel so much better!

Becoming You

What are you doing now that just doesn't feel right? Are you in a relationship that makes you feel less than you are? Are you working at a job that doesn't energize you? Perhaps you are playing an instrument when you would rather be writing your first novel?

If what you are doing doesn't feel good to you, then you are not on the path to happiness. Try these **Simple Steps** to redirect your energy:

- Create a three-column list. In one column, write down what you love to do and are actually doing. In the next column, write what you love to do and aren't doing. In the last column, write down what you are doing that doesn't feel good to you.

- Look at the items in the last column ... the ones that don't feel so good. Cross out anything you can stop doing right now. Stop doing them! For things you can't stop doing immediately, decide which items in your other two columns you could substitute for them.

- Pick one of these items to change and devise your conversion plan. If it means you need to learn a new skill, look into schools or mentors who can help you. Use your evenings to learn those skills. When you are ready ... convert!

Remember: it's YOUR choice! No one gets to decide what makes you happy. That's entirely up to you. Redirect your energy to what makes you happy!

How Do You Define Yourself?

When you are asked who you are, how do you respond? Do you define yourself by your marital status, your job, as a parent? Do you see yourself through your accomplishments? Or do you describe yourself by some event in your life?

You probably have friends that refer to themselves as "losers," "unlovable" and even "stupid." What we call ourselves is how we see ourselves. As long as we stay steeped in negativity, that's all we experience.

For those of you who are trying to find **Real Change** in your life ... how are these labels working for you?

Remember:

- Every time we say we're "challenged," we are.

- Every time we think we're "a failure," we are.

- Every time we think we're "resourceful," we are.

- Every time we think we're "loved," we are.

We become what we think about, so why not start with thinking the best of ourselves?

When you catch yourself thinking something negative about yourself, try this **Simple Step** and discover the **Real Change**!

- Stop. Say "NO! That thought doesn't serve me. I am not that person. I am resourceful/loved/creative/smart/happy" (fill in the positive words that describe who you really are).

- Repeat every single time the negativity creeps into your head.

When we change how we think about ourselves, we change our lives. It's that **Simple**! And it feels great!

It's Your Time to Decide

When I was young, I thought I knew better than just about anyone ... especially anyone over the age of thirty.

Now, after years of trials and tribulations and just living this long ... I've come to realize two things. First, I have nothing to prove to anyone anymore, and second, I have nothing to lose by speaking my mind ... or not. I also recognize that regardless of what happens to me in my life, I will survive - and probably thrive – in the good times and not so good. This is a good place to be ... a place of peace.

Where are you in your life? Are you dependent on another person's guidance? Do you seek approval from family, friends and coworkers? Or are you secure knowing that you know what you know and that you're good at what you do?

If you haven't quite made it to that place where you are honestly secure and self-assured, try these **Simple Steps** to move closer to your authentic self:

- Start making small decisions without anyone's input. Decide what to have for dinner or what you are going to wear when you go to your reunion. As you start trusting your judgment on the little things ... you'll gain the confidence to take it up a notch.

- If you are facing what you consider to be a big decision, such as taking a job in another city or buying a car, do your research. Don't leave it to fate ... or emotions. For example: I really wanted to move back to the Pacific Northwest. I didn't want to throw caution and planning to the wind - that could be a financial disaster. Instead, I planned each step and made sure I accounted for each one before I sold off my furniture and signed a contract for a moving company.

- If the decision is really major and requires expertise (legal, financial, medical), determine who the experts are in the field. Make an appointment for a consultation. Go prepared with questions. Take a notebook to write down answers and information. If you can, record the conversation so you can review it again later. Follow up questions can always be sent via e-mail or during a phone call. Never allow yourself to feel pressured to make a decision until you are ready. When you feel you are well prepared to make the decision, make it!

Regardless of the decision you make, there is this really cool factor to remember: nothing is permanent. If circumstances change in the future, you can make a new decision. Knowing that makes the process less scary. And that is true freedom!

Desire It!

Know What You Want

At the center of your being you have the answer;
you know who you are and
you know what you want.

— Lao Tzu

Desire It!
Know What You Want

Introduction

I am sitting on a rock at Bandon Beach on the Oregon Coast as Jack begins his first round of photography for the day. At a distance I can see him in the surf with a backpack, tripod and camera, getting down into the frigid water just to get the perfect angle for the shot. Three hours from now he will return to the same spot, hoping to capture the rock formations in the perfect light.

Jack knows what he wants ... even more ... he will pursue it relentlessly until he gets what he wants. What about you? Do you know what you want? Are you prepared to sacrifice what you have for what you want?

I admire Jack's tenacity when it comes to photography. And I admire those kids in school who seemed to know what they wanted to be when they grew up. It's that drive and singular focus that enables them to succeed, regardless of adversity, detractors and roadblocks. When you know what you want and have the passion necessary to turn it into your reality ... you do!

If you are reading this chapter, then you probably aren't where you want to be when it comes to doing what you love. You are not alone! I was in my fifties before I figured it out. It came as a quiet discovery - not a startling revelation. And as quietly as it arrived, it took me a while longer to even realize that what I had wanted was right in front of me all along.

In this chapter I'm going to give you a few **Simple Steps** that will help you hone in on what you want. Since everyone receives information differently, there are a variety of options for you to experiment with. Not every **Simple Step** will be appropriate for your situation ... yet each one offers ideas that can help you determine what you want out of life.

It's really important to take the time to figure out what is important to you. If you just let life happen, then you have to take whatever comes your way. What if you don't like it? Are you going to keep waiting and hoping for a

125

different result?

You don't have to pile on the pressure to figure out your "calling." When, however, you focus on what brings you joy, you'll discover your future is actually calling you.

If you're ready to start living your life by your own design, turn the page and take a **Simple Step** forward.

Do What You Love

Are you doing what you love? Or are you doing what you do out of a sense of responsibility or duty? Are you happy to get up and go to work most days? Or do you dread another day of work?

If you could start all over again, what would you choose to do for your life's work? Is something keeping you from taking that path?

The days of working for one company all your life are a thing of the past. Like me, you could be out of a job tomorrow if your company is acquired. You can start right now to pursue your dream. You don't have to quit your current job, and you don't have to give up the lifestyle you enjoy. Just take a **Simple Step** toward your dream ... toward your happiness.

These **Simple Steps** will help you get clear about pursuing your dream:

- Create two columns on a spreadsheet or notepad. On the left side, write down everything you can think of that you enjoy doing. On the right side, list those things you know you're good at.

- Compare the two columns. What appears in both? Circle it. It's all right if you don't find something in both columns. Look for those items that are similar. For example: you may love to read, and you may be good at critiquing or proof reading your son's term paper. Connect similar ideas with a line or circle.

- Take the circled or lined items and write them down on a clean sheet of paper. Fold it up and take it with you wherever you go. When you're waiting in line or taking a break, pull it out and just look at it. As you do this, your mind will start creating an image of you in a new role that plays to your passion and your talents.

When you create an image in your mind that brings that sparkle to your eye ... you will know that you are on the right path ... for you!

Find Your Purpose

All of us want to find our purpose. We get to a point in life when we want to know why we are here.

The key to finding your purpose lies in determining what you are passionate about. While that may seem like an easy thing to do ... it's not. Throughout my life I've always wanted to help people, and when I did that, it made me happy. I didn't realize, however, that it was my purpose until about a year later.

When you do something that excites you, and you're willing to pursue it relentlessly, you have discovered your purpose. It may take time to hone in on exactly what that purpose looks like, but that's ok. Life's a journey and enjoying the sights along the way only makes it better.

Try these **Simple Steps** and begin to identify your purpose:

- Ask those closest to you (family, friends, coworkers) to write down what they think you do best. You're looking for that top line item. Don't look at the responses and ask them not to tell you.

- Ask yourself what you enjoy most above anything else you do. Make your list and then look at what is written by others. Where is the commonality?

As you look at the lists, what "calls" to you? If there's more than one thing, that's ok. Your purpose may involve a combination of choices. Create a list of items that feels right to you. Keep that list with you at all times.

What you've done with these **Simple Steps** is to put in motion the energy that surrounds your purpose.

As you think about what you have written, visualize what it means to you. Watch as the synchronicities develop, and before you know it, you'll be living your dream!

Can You See Your Dreams?

Are you a dreamer? Did you know what you wanted to be when you grew up? Could you see yourself doing it?

For most of my life I couldn't dream. I wasn't one of those girls who saw Prince Charming on his white horse ... nor could I see what I wanted to be when I grew up. Dreaming was for people who didn't take responsibility. It was capricious, and of course, any dreamer was out of touch with the real world ... or so I thought.

Fast forward to today. Most of us have family, children, job, pets ... we have responsibilities that we've chosen, and sometimes we let them get in the way of our dreams.

When you reach outside your responsibilities and push yourself to visualize the future ... try to imagine there are no limitations and that what you see is 100 percent within your power to achieve.

Once you can really see your future and your dreams ... you can focus on them and make decisions that bring them into reality.

If you want to make a commitment to your dreams, try these **Simple Steps** to crystallize them:

- Define your passion. Write down what you love to do. A passion is something you would ignore everything else in order to do. You may have more than one passion. Start with the one that's at the core of all the others ... or the one that speaks the loudest to you! In my case, my passion is helping others find happiness.

- Now that you know what your passion is ... dig down deeper and figure out what it is about your passion that means the most. Using me as an example: what means the most to me is helping others to see the positive aspects of their lives and the power of living in that positive place.

131

- Next, list the opportunities that come with that refined passion. For me it includes: our website, our Facebook page, writing books which provide **Simple Steps** to happiness, developing social programs including webinars and seminars, etc.

- Spend a few hours reflecting on items on the list that you want to pursue and decide when you want to do them. Your gut feelings can assist you with this. For me, the website, the first book and the Facebook page began my journey to my dream.

- Now, memorialize your plan and keep it with you at all times. Refer to it often. As you come upon decision points in your life, ask if your dreams will materialize quicker with each choice you make.

Here's the bottom line: if all your senses are consumed by your dream ... it's going to come true. Make the decision right now to be the creator of your dream ... not a bystander in life.

Change Your Focus

If you believe in the Law of Attraction, then you know there's no lack in the world. Everything you desire is waiting for you … if you are open to receiving it. All it takes is focus.

Are you focusing on what you really want in your life – your goals and dreams - or are you focusing on what you don't have? For example: have you always wanted financial abundance and yet you continually talk about not having enough money? As long as you focus on the lack of money … that's what the Universe will provide.

When you realize what your focus is and become grateful for the abundance you do have … things start happening. It's magic.

If you are focusing on something that is lacking in your life, try these **Simple Steps** to change your thoughts:

- Identify what is the most important quality of your life (i.e., family, relationships, money, work).

- Write down what comes to mind, what you think about this quality. Does your focus reflect that you don't have something? If it does, you are focusing on the lack. For example, if you haven't had a good date lately, do you complain that there are no available good men or women?

- If your focus is on the lack of something … restate it to a positive. If you said "There aren't any good men or women around," try changing it to "I haven't found someone I want to date again. However, each person I've met has shown me the characteristics in a partner that are important to me. I'm not going to settle for less!"

Pay attention to your thoughts. When you focus on the positive aspects of your life, you experience more good things coming your way. Try it!

Channel Your Thoughts

Do you have days when sorting through all the thoughts that pop into your brain leave you feeling overwhelmed? Do you wonder how to cut through what's viable and what isn't?

We have over sixty thousand thoughts every day. No wonder we have trouble focusing!

When your thoughts are overtaking your ability to think, try these **Simple Steps**:

- Write down every single thought.

- As you write, if you're laughing at the thought AND you have zero interest in what you have written, cross it off.

- Rewrite and organize what's left on your list.

- Now walk away. It's all there in writing ... you don't have to think it through. Give yourself a chance to be distracted. Play with your kids, call a friend, walk your dog ... anything to take your mind to a more relaxing place.

- When you are ready, go back to your list. Is there something that jumps out at you? Do you feel a strong connection to anything in particular? If you do, then go with it. If you don't, shred the list ... leave it to your Higher Power to address.

When you organize what matters and throw out what doesn't, you begin to focus on what is important to you. And isn't that what you really want to do?

Focus on What You Want

Dreams and desires sit out on the horizon without a plan to achieve them. We see them, but they're like the pot of gold at the end of the rainbow ... unreachable.

There's no magic carpet ride to nirvana.

When we make a plan and make a concerted effort to work that plan, our dreams move into our reality ... possibility becomes probability!

We don't have to know all the details, and that's ok ... some parts we may just need to leave to a Higher Power to provide.

Try these **Simple Steps** to determine what you need to do and what you don't:

- Make a list of all the things on your plate. Include what's there now and what needs to be done in the next thirty days.

- To the right of your list make three columns. Mark them "Me," "Someone Else" and "Higher Power." The "Someone Else" column needs to be wide enough to mark in a name or initials of the "Someone Else."

- Now, go through your list and check the:

  o "Me" box for anything you absolutely have to do yourself. Include in here anything you love to do! For example, if you are due for your annual physical, you can't delegate that one any more than you can delegate writing a term paper. If you love to tend to your garden, then this one is yours too.

  o "Someone Else" box for any task you don't have to do, don't want to do or don't love to do. Examples may include:

organizing a bake sale at church, bathing the dog or washing your college son's laundry.

- o "Higher Power" box. Put anything in here that didn't make it onto your priority list in the first place or that you aren't required by law or your livelihood to do. Examples might be: planning where you're going to stay on your driving vacation, figuring out how you're going to fit fifty people into your home for a party or even figuring out how you're going to physically move your household across country.

Once you've removed those tasks that really don't have to be on your plate, you can focus on what's important to you … your dreams and your happiness. Move forward in the direction of your dreams, and they become your reality.

What Defines You

Parents tend to define themselves by their children: "I'm Sarah's mom" or "My children go to the Fulton School." Some people identify themselves by the church they attend. And you know there are folks who give credit for who they are to the college they attended. We define ourselves by our jobs, our religion, our family and even our mistakes.

Are you your illness? Your financial status? A portion of a relationship? Have you defined yourself over the years as "not worthy," "overweight," "stupid," "capable but not privileged" - a failure?

When I was working, I defined myself by my accomplishments. In the last few years, I found myself identifying with my perceived failures: unemployment, financial stress and physical condition. I am, however, none of those things ... they are merely experiences in my life's journey. And in those experiences are the lessons that make me the person I am today ... not a judgment of myself.

When we define ourselves as something less than we want to be, it's usually because of a comment by a friend or authority figure (parent, spouse, boss). We take their perception to heart because we somehow believe that another's opinion matters more than our own. Are you tied down by that definition?

How we define ourselves can influence the things we do in life. Maybe it's time to change how you see yourself. Step outside your comfort zone and paint a new picture ... leave behind all the external monikers and create the image of the person you know you're destined to be. Your new image will attract those events into your life that take you in the direction of your dreams.

When you're ready to build your new self-image, try these **Simple Steps:**

- Be still and listen. When we learn to be still and listen to our soul, we can press past the exterior perceptions and get in touch with our true selves.

Some definitions can be wiped out in a heartbeat ... others may take years of perseverance to overcome ... still others may require the assistance of a professional.

- Tend to yourself. Try doing things that help you get in touch with your true nature: outdoor exercise, dance, yoga, tai chi.

- Laugh. Belly laughter comes from the gut. Your gut feelings can help you know what's true and false in your life.

- Be true to yourself. Create an affirmation that supports the new you.

Once you make the decision to be the person you want to be, you will realize you were that person all along. All you needed was to take your first step.

Don't Stop Living Because of Stress

Stress is part of life ... sometimes it can be too big a part. What is it you love doing but aren't doing because life got in the way? Fess up! Come clean ... at least with yourself.

It seems like the things we love to do are the first things we give up when we're stressed out. We create so many legitimate reasons why we can't do what we enjoy doing ... when the truth is, if we'd focus on what we love to do, our stress would be less.

When you're facing challenges, what do you quit doing? Does your healthy diet or daily walk fall off your plate? Do you stop socializing with your good friends because you don't want them to know what you're going through? Does the work you love get marginalized because of something going on at home? (Or vice versa?)

Sure, there are issues that might have to take priority, but they don't have to take an eternity.

Too much stress in our lives can stop us dead in our tracks ... we stop moving forward toward our dreams and goals. When you're ready to get back to being the best you can be, try one of these **Simple Steps**:

- Turn off the television. Take that thirty to sixty minutes of mindless time to meditate, soak in a tub, take a walk ... anything that gives you quiet, personal time. Get back in touch with you.

- Make a list of activities or people that need your attention. Limit the list to three - no need to add stress if you don't get to it. Now, prioritize. Take the first item and take action. Don't hesitate ... no excuses. Once you have the first one completed, go to the next. When you are done with all three, try the first **Simple Step** (again, maybe) and take time for you.

- Ask a friend or family member to be your reality check. Use someone who knows you well ... and cares about you. When they see you withdrawing or faltering, ask them to give you a loving nudge. Make a commitment to pay attention when they do. This also works great if the two of you are helping each other!

Life is meant to be lived. We all know that. We just forget it when Life gets in the way of living. Make a promise to yourself to make each day of your life count. It's about you ... your now!

Stalled?

You've been moving forward toward your dream when suddenly you realize you've come to a screeching halt. It's like your wheels are spinning and you're stuck.

We all go through times in our lives when we feel like that. We've landed in a rut, and no matter what we do, we can't seem to get it into gear.

Do you find yourself coming up with every excuse in the book not to take a **Simple Step** forward? Our dreams can wait ... but why should they? We seem to make everything and everyone else a priority ... even when our friends and family encourage us to take care of ourselves.

What is it that's keeping our lives in neutral?

Only you can create the life of your dreams ... so if you aren't living your dream ... it's because you choose not to.

Hmmmm ... What are you waiting for?

Take a **Simple Step** today ... just one. Take ten minutes and commit to paper what your dream is. That's it. Easy ... and **Simple**. Describe your dream ... use details so you can see and feel what your life will be like when you achieve it.

Your time is now....

Changing Is a Choice

Everyone wants to change ... we just don't think it's easy. There are many reasons for thinking that way, from not being able to let go of something that happened in the past to being afraid of getting hurt to just not trusting anymore.

When we have lived in pain for so long, making any change isn't easy. There's no light switch we can flip to make it all go away.

If someone tells you to "get over it," they probably aren't the best person to be supporting you. They don't know what it's like to walk in your shoes. What they see externally may be the tip of an iceberg.

When you are personally ready to make a change ... you will. Sometimes it takes reaching a point of unbearable pain to be motivated enough to move forward.

We can choose between being happy and being miserable. Sometimes misery works. However, when you're miserable enough, you'll get to that critical mass point and make a new decision. And because you felt the pain, you'll appreciate being pain free even more.

If you need some help moving quickly through your misery, try one of these **Simple Steps**:

- Spend one day wallowing in your misery. Complain to anyone who will listen. Cry if that works for you. Write down all the reasons why you're miserable. Observe how people react to you. Assess how you feel throughout the day. Now ask yourself if this is the person you want to be?

- As you pass by a mirror, notice how you look. This isn't about vanity, it's about the expression on your face, the drawn look and the slump of your shoulders. This is how being miserable looks. Is this the way you want to look?

- List out all your friends and family. Who have you seen or spoken to lately? Has your list become smaller since you've been miserable? Is this the life you want to live?

When you look at the cost of your misery and realize all that is lost by your choice, you'll make another choice. Make it the choice to be happy. It feels so much better!

Empower Yourself

How often do you find yourself waiting until someone or something in your life changes before you do what you want to do?

"After the holidays, I'll start my diet."

"When I get another job, I'll be happy."

"When my son moves out of the house, I'll start ... (pick a creative endeavor)."

As long as we delay starting ... our dreams remain in that "someday" place. It's time to lose the "all or none" thoughts and take a **Simple Step** toward your dream.

Try one of these **Simple Steps** to help you move forward:

•Need to Do:

> ◦ Make a list of the actions you need to take in order to achieve your dream.

> ◦ Break each action down into the smallest components.

> ◦ Now, prioritize and take one of those little steps.

> For example: if you want to write a book, you need to have a concept, an outline of the chapters, an introduction and an "about the author" page.

> ◦ Pick one and start writing. You don't have to do it all at once!

•Need NOT to Do:

∘ Make a list of all the roadblocks you believe are keeping you from accomplishing your dream.

Let's say you want to start your own business. You're working full-time, taking care of your kids and perhaps your parents, arranging the family social calendar and it's holiday time.

∘ Determine which of these responsibilities you can turn over to a Higher Power to handle.

∘ Communication is the key with this **Simple Step**. Tell your friends and family what your goal is and ask them to help.

∘ Delegate what you can to others and resist any instincts to take over when something isn't going as you would normally do it!

∘ The time you free up can be used to take one of your smaller steps from above and start working on your dream!

It's easy to let life get in the way of your dreams. Turn the tide, and let your dreams get in the way of your life! When that happens ... you'll discover that life is living your dreams!

See It!

Visualize

Visualize this thing that you want,
see it, feel it, believe in it.
Make your mental blue print, and begin to build.
— Robert Collier

See It! Visualize

Introduction

Picture the most beautiful place in the world that you long to visit. See yourself enjoying the scenery and the adventure of this location. Feel the climate, smell the air and use every sense you have to experience what it would be like if you were there right now. You've just visualized your dream.

Visualization enables you to experience what you want to do, be or have. It focuses your attention on what you want and allows you to experience it "as if" you had it right now. By frequently keeping your dreams in front of you, feeling them in your mind, heart and soul, you begin to make decisions that take you in the direction of that dream.

I was raised to live in the "real world" ... daydreaming was irresponsible. It took me years to be able to allow myself the luxury of dreaming. Even then, I needed all the help I could get in picturing what I wanted my life to be like. When I took the time to visualize what I wanted, and repeated that often, my dreams became my reality.

You've probably watched Olympic skiers preparing for their run down the mountain. They'll stand in wait for their turn, eyes closed, their bodies moving as they see themselves encountering every twist and turn. That's what you need to do right now to start moving forward toward your dream.

It doesn't take long or really much effort to envision your dream. A few minutes throughout your day is all you need to put the wheels in motion. How you visualize, though, is up to you.

Painting your dream picture is a very personal choice. While some are comfortable sitting back for a few minutes and seeing their new life in their mind's eye, others need more physical props. In this chapter we'll talk about vision boards and mind movies, in addition to the process of acting "as if."

When you see your dream coming true, it will. When you believe in the power of your dreams, you turn them into your reality. If you're ready to take a **Simple Step** forward, read on!

You Hold Your World in Your Hands

Visualize a small little globe sitting in the palm of your hand. You hold in your hand every aspect of your life and how you choose to live it. It is that close, that manageable ... and mostly yours to do with as you please.

It's up to you how you create your world. Work, family life, hobbies, recreation, relationships ... anything that involves you is yours to do with as you choose. Just a bit of clarification here: this doesn't mean that I believe you choose your parents or an abusive relationship or to be sick. Events occur in our lives without any input from us; how we choose to react or deal with them is 100 percent in our control.

You alone have the power to be happy. No one "makes" you happy. That is your responsibility. The reverse is also true. You may not like what someone else does; however, they can't force you to be unhappy. The choice is yours.

Spend a few minutes every day visualizing the world you want to create for yourself. What does it look like? Who is in it? What brings you joy? When you reinforce your dreams by visualizing them, you often start making decisions which change them from a dream to your reality.

Clear Your Path

Are you your own worst enemy?

If you are trying to lose weight, do you sabotage your plan in a New York minute? Do you go to extremes and try to get to your goal as fast as you can, only to give up a few days into it? Or do you make excuses for why you bought the potato chips from the vending machine, rather than eating the orange in your lunch? Either way, you have doomed yourself.

Rather than our own biggest supporter, we tend to be our own harshest critic.

What are you doing to drive a wedge between you and your goals?

When you realize that you alone are hampering your progress, try this **Simple Step** to get yourself out of your way:

- Identify a self-defeating habit that trips you up. For example: raiding the vending machines at work.

- Write that behavior down on a note card or print it out.

- Now, take a big red marker and draw a circle around the behavior and draw a line through it.

- Post it where you will see it at the time you are most likely to act on it.

A not so subtle reminder becomes a strong motivator to support you! Once you have made it past that first hurdle, choose another. When you take things one **Simple Step** at a time, you'll realize how easy positive change is!

Be Still

In the middle of the night when I'm wide awake, I think back on my life. I have my fair share of regrets, but dwelling on them doesn't do me any good. I acknowledge them and let them go.

Throughout my life I've always wanted to help people, but it took losing my job to find myself. Things happen for a reason.

You've heard that your Higher Power doesn't give you anymore than you can handle ... but sometimes, don't you wish he didn't trust you so much? You just want to cut to the chase and realize your dreams. It is, however, in the experiences you are navigating that your dreams take form.

If you find yourself being impatient for your dreams to come true, I encourage you to take a **Simple Step** with me.

- Devote fifteen minutes to being still. This is a challenge for some. Your family, work and thoughts will test your resolve. In being still you release the stress of your week ... or your life ... if only for a little while.

- Tune into your dream ... experience your life as if you were living your dream right now. Feel the excitement, the joy, the contentment. See yourself as you dream your life to be. In these few moments dedicated to you and your dream, you begin to draw the energy of the universe into your dream, and it begins to form around you.

As you return to your normal pace, do so knowing that your life is proceeding just as it needs to, and your dream is on its way. Repeat this **Simple Step** often and you accelerate the process ... all the while you are practicing patience by being still.

Believe in Yourself

Believing in yourself is a key component in getting to where you want to be. So many people know you're capable, yet you doubt yourself. It's that doubt that needs to be wiped out of your memory bank.

Doubt isn't something that just showed up when we started examining our dreams. It's been dogging us for a long time. Every time we shy away from trying something new - socializing, speaking in front of people we don't know - that little (ok, not so little) aggravating thing called "doubt" creeps into our heads. We don't even get into gear because it's there nagging at us.

The best way to get rid of doubt is through action. If we are going to live the dream, then we have to banish doubt.

Try this **Simple Step**:

- Do something you haven't done before. You get to decide how bold you want to be. It might be as simple as walking an extra block or calling up someone you would like to have as a mentor. How much you do and how dramatic your actions are is totally up to you.

The key here is to do something that you've been shying away from because of doubt. Once you do, you'll realize it wasn't as big a deal as your mind had you believing. Now you'll have the confidence to try something else.

Remember to keep visualizing your dreams throughout your day and work on overcoming your doubt. With each **Simple Step** you take, you are one step closer to your dream.

Feel Your Dream

Let's talk about your dream.

Do you feel your dream with every cell in your body?

Can you feel it, taste it, smell it?

You might not be there quite yet. Perhaps you're thinking you want it, but it will never happen ... or you don't know HOW to make it happen.

If you think it will never happen, then realize you're setting yourself up for failure before you even take your first step. If you don't believe it with every cell in your body, then you're not ready to pursue it. Now, that said, you're not alone if you feel that way. We've been so conditioned to "face reality" that anything that seems like a dream is considered "for the birds."

Here's the real truth: reality is what you decide it should be .... not what someone else tells you it is. This is all about you and your dreams. How many successful people were told they could never do what they wanted ... and yet they did exactly what they said they would!?! That's what we have to do if we're going to achieve our dreams.

Now ... if you don't know "how" you're going to make your dream come true, that's ok! It's enough to start by feeling your dream with your body and soul. When you do that, you are telling your Higher Power that you're ready ... and your Higher Power will deliver!

Get Excited

When you take a **Simple Step** in the direction of your dreams, you put positive energy in motion, and it grows exponentially! Even better, you generate a level of excitement that propels you even further.

Here are a few **Simple Steps** you can take that will advance you in the direction of your dream:

- General:

    o Find an appealing looking box or container. Label it (or not) your "Anything Contained Within - Is" box. As you focus on your dreams, write down specifics that are important to you. Whether it's a diamond ring, new home, relationship or fame and fortune ... put them in your box and move on. (In mine I have pictures of where I want to live, clothes I want to fit into and one of Jack in great health living a long life.)

- Job Related:

    o Create or update your resume. Even if you like your current position, you should always have your resume ready.
    o Set up job searches that will e-mail you when target jobs in your field and location come available.

- Health Related:

    o Set up an appointment with your doctor for a physical. Talk to her about your goals and ask for help. She can give you resource information to consider, or specific directions.

    o If you are trying to lose or gain weight, consider reading *You on a Diet* by Mehmet Oz. He and his coauthor have a terrific tongue-in-cheek approach. Check the book out of the library or go to Half Price Books to pick up your own copy.

- o   If you want to be more physically active, decide what you want to be able to do. Whether it's walking, biking, hiking or skydiving, start your research online. Figure out who the experts are and read their pages or blogs.

- Relationship Related:

  - o   If you are in a serious relationship and want to enhance it … decide what attributes you want to improve. Pick the one that means the most to you and talk to your partner about it. Once you open up the dialogue, you may just find your partner wants the same thing, too. As you start sharing … decide together what your first step is.

  - o   If you are in an unsupportive relationship, determine if you can open up that dialogue from above. If you can, go for it! If you can't … try putting your thoughts in a letter or e-mail and sending it to your partner. Only you can decide if you want to continue in an unsupportive relationship.

  - o   If you are searching for that "perfect for you" partner, make a list of the attributes that you want. When you are done, take a few moments and visualize the relationship. Now, put it away. You have set your intention. Let your Higher Power take it from there.

Whether one of these **Simple Steps** works for you, or you have others … the point is to move forward in the direction of your dream.

Internalize Happiness

There is nothing outside ourselves that can ever "make" us happy. All the stuff, the money, the job - even other people - don't result in lasting happiness. Alternately, we can make ourselves truly miserable when we focus on what's missing in our lives.

Are you looking for and finding the good things in your life ... or are you focusing on what isn't? When you realize that happiness exists within you, you will never again search for it in others, or by accumulating "stuff."

Try this **Simple Step** to find the happiness within you:

- Sit quietly where you won't be disturbed. Close the door, take a bath or drive to a quiet park.

- Close your eyes and take two or three deep breaths.

- Imagine a beautiful white light flowing through your scalp into your brain. Now, feel it as it infuses every cell of your body with gentle warmth. Slowly allow yourself to smile.

- When you are ready, open your eyes. Sit quietly and take in the sense of peace that you created through this **Simple Step**.

In a few short moments, with very little effort, you can take yourself to a place of peacefulness. When you realize you can do this all by yourself ... you know without a doubt that you are the sole creator of your happiness!

Visualize the Life of Your Dreams

Do you love watching the Olympics? Do you live vicariously through the passion of these athletes? Watch the skiers as they stand at the top of the hill, close their eyes and ski the run in their mind. Those who can visualize their success, achieve it.

The same is true for non-athletes. Visualization works for every part of your life. When you "see" your dream, you achieve it! And the more time you spend in that place, the closer you are to living it.

All it takes is a few seconds focused on your dream - repeatedly, consistently - to move it into your reality.

Are you ready to take a cue from our Olympic athletes? Try this **Simple Step** to create the focus necessary to realize your dreams:

- Write out a clear description of your dream. Break it into short manageable sections. When you are done, read it out loud to yourself. The goal here is to make sure you are clear about your dream.

- Sit quietly where you won't be disturbed for at least five minutes.

- Work with one section at a time.

- Close your eyes and picture the first section of your dream. Spend at least seventeen seconds visualizing what the words represent and repeat them in your mind. The longer you can spend on each section the more real it will feel.

- Work through each section until you have painted the full image of your dream in your mind.

- Repeat daily, or more often if you can.

The more "real" you make your dream through visualization … the more you can see it, feel it and even taste it … the faster you realize it!

Create a Vision Board

Visualization uses the imagination and empowers us to "see" our dreams. There are no limits ... the more open we are, and the bigger we dare to see, the greater are our possibilities.

If you believe in the Law of Attraction, then you know that the universe lines up with what we visualize.

Try these **Simple Steps** to create a Vision Board to keep your dreams in front of you:

- A Vision Board is a giant poster that depicts your dreams. You can use a bulletin board, poster board or any large flat surface. It is important that you like how this base for your Vision Board looks. You will be looking at it often.

- Cut out or print photos or images that represent your dreams or goals. For example: if you dream of traveling the world, include images that represent the places you are going to.

- Add quotes, affirmations or phrases that mean something to you. Using the travel example, you may relate to the words "I jet to faraway places often."

- As you pull together the images and words that "speak" to you, secure them to your Vision Board in a way that is appealing.

- Place your Vision Board where you will see it often. The more you look at your board, the more powerful it is.

When you visualize your dreams and keep those images where you see them, you'll make decisions that support your dreams. Every **Simple Step** you take is a step forward!

Act "As If"

We all have those days when we want to crawl back under the covers and hide from the world to regroup or re-energize and relax.

When your day turns into a week or longer, then it's time to reconsider exactly what is going on in your life. If there is some major stress (death, job loss, financial failure, the end of a relationship, etc.), then you may need to seek additional support from a professional. Or you may just need to cut yourself a break and give yourself the time to heal.

Perhaps those events are in the distant past and you really haven't had anything major go wrong recently. Maybe it seems like nothing is going the way you want it to ... it may be a great time to act "as if!"

According to Abraham-Hicks: "Once you activate a vibration within you, the Law of Attraction begins responding to that vibration, and you're off and running."

If you are ready to move into a more positive space, then it's time to generate a vibration that supports you. Try one of these **Simple Steps** to take on the role of your lifetime:

- Dress up! This one is simple. Pull out those special clothes you only wear to church or a special event. Go out to lunch with a friend or just walk through a mall or park. There is no easier way to feel better than to know you look marvelous!

- If there is a situation you need to be strong for, script out what you want to say or accomplish. Stand in front of a mirror and practice your role. When you practice, you are prepared. You can anticipate different reactions and determine ahead of time what your response will be.

- Practice visualization. Think of this as a personal movie script of your life. Close your eyes and picture how you would look and act in the life of your dreams. Feel the emotion, excitement and love that you experience when you are living the life of your dreams. Practice this often.

In each of these **Simple Steps** you are generating the positive vibration that attracts your dreams into your life. As you get more comfortable acting "as if" you want your life to be, you'll discover that what was an act has become your reality!

Give It!

Be Thankful

All that we behold is full of blessings.

– William Wordworth

Give It! Be Thankful

Introduction

The power of a simple "Thank You" goes beyond words. The sincere expression of gratitude is all it takes to show another that you appreciate them. Whether someone has held a door open for you or given you their attention, acknowledging their kindness and their effort reinforces their behavior ... and yours.

Your thanks is more valuable than any gift you could give. It's not about the cost ... it's about the sentiment. You know how good you feel when someone appreciates what you've done. Whether it comes in a note or in person, you've been recognized for your kindness and assistance.

Giving thanks extends beyond the expression to another person. When you give thanks for what is going on in your life, right now, you send a message to your Higher Power that you appreciate your life. It's through your gratitude that you acknowledge the blessings in your life ... even if they come in the form of challenges.

No matter how difficult your life may be, gratitude for the experience exudes positive energy. It's not that you want more unhappiness, but that you understand what's going on contains a lesson. Expressing gratitude for the lesson can turn a difficult situation into an encouraging experience.

Every day we experience beauty and miracles. As simple as a good cup of coffee in the morning or your child's hug as they head out the door to school ... these little joys envelop our lives. Take nothing for granted in life. Instead ... recognize it and give thanks.

Now, imagine what your life would be like if you were sincerely grateful for every moment? With gratitude comes peace because you know that whatever comes your way happens for a reason. You may not always know what the reason is, or understand the long-range effects, but deep inside your soul you know your life is progressing as it needs to.

Gratitude ... Feel it, Live it, Express it! When you do, amazing things will happen in your life!

Banish the Blues

It takes time to realize a dream. "Instantaneous" isn't in the Law of Attraction's vocabulary. It's about seeing and acting "as if" and then watching as your dream materializes. It's about the journey, not the destination.

Sometimes, however, the journey gets to you, and the "blues" hit. If you find yourself in that blue funk state ... the only way out is to focus on something outside yourself.

Try these **Simple Steps** to turn your blues into a more positive state of mind:

- Give thanks. Whether you say it out loud or write it down, spend five minutes doing nothing except being grateful. When you realize how much you have to be thankful for, your attitude will begin to shift. Do this several times a day depending on your state of mind.

- Help someone else. Make cookies for your kids or an elderly neighbor. Do a chore that your spouse normally does that he/she doesn't enjoy.

- Go for a walk. Take your dog for a walk. Whether you go alone or take others along with you, getting out in the fresh air will do you good. As you walk, notice the beauty around you and give thanks for that too.

We all get down now and then. Don't beat yourself up if you're there ... give yourself the time you need to heal. Give thanks for the blessings you do have in your life and nudge your focus back to the positive side of life.

Dare to Reach

It's easy to get caught up in our daily lives and overlook another who needs help. Help may be a smile, a kind word or simply the opportunity to be heard.

Kindness is the greatest gift. Giving without expecting anything in return is the purest blessing you can give. In giving freely you generate positive energy that extends far beyond the person you help. It extends to the energy around them ... and then ripples out into the universe.

Today's **Simple Step** is to help another. This one is both easy and simple. Be a friend, practice a random act of kindness, volunteer to help where needed.

Your kindness will reach far and wide, and your soul will be filled with joy and love for those you've helped. And that feels great!

Everyday Joys

Trees in bloom, warmer weather, going barefoot ... these little joys bring a renewed sense of hope for me. I see possibilities, and nuisances and aggravations give way to peacefulness.

Our lives get so hectic sometimes that we don't stop to smell the roses or watch the birds fly. The truth is, we have the time. It just takes a willingness to step off the merry-go-round that is daily life ... and simply breathe.

Try these **Simple Steps** when you are ready to experience everyday events as the joys that they are:

- Walk away from your computer or cell phone or IPad. Take a few minutes and sit on your porch or walk down your driveway. Notice the budding leaves and the grass turning green.

- Go buy ice cream! As the temperature warms up, there's nothing better than that first taste of your favorite flavor.

- Drive with your windows down, your moon roof or convertible open. Breathe in the clean, fresh spring air.

- Take your first leisurely bike ride around the neighborhood.

Today is about the promise that little joys bring! Be thankful for everyone and most of all - Enjoy!

Find Peace Now

Don't you love those times when there's balance in your life? Tomorrow may be crazy with work - "to do's" and responsibilities - but right now, just for a few moments, all is right with the world and nothing else matters.

Have you ever had those moments when you want to freeze time ... when the only thing that matters is now? The past and future fall away, and living in this moment shines.

If you're looking to capture this kind of peace in your life, try this **Simple Step** to help focus on the now:

- Plan fifteen or twenty minutes each week (or each day if you can) that will be your time. It may be after you've put the kids to bed or while you're alone. What's important is that you have quiet time.

- Now, close your eyes and listen to your surroundings. Pick one sound that is peaceful to you. It may be the sound of the breeze through the trees or even the hum of your furnace.

- As you breathe gently, focus all your attention on that sound. Let it be the din that envelops you. As thoughts pop into your head, acknowledge them and refocus on your sound.

- Spend a few minutes in this place. When you are ready to move on, give thanks for the peacefulness.

Enjoy how refreshed you feel after taking these few moments for yourself. It's in this time that you will recognize your power to live in the "now" and the blessing that is to your life.

When You Give, You Receive

Did you give any thought ... or even better ... take any action to help someone else today? This act is truly one of the best life changers you can undertake. Taking your focus off your challenges by helping another provides much-needed perspective. When you give to another without expectation of receiving anything back, you discover that your kindness is returned to you.

Try these **Simple Steps** when you are ready to focus your energy on helping others. Remember: you don't have to spend a dime ... you just need to give your time. An hour a week can make a difference in your life and the lives of those who are touched by your kindness.

- Offer to mow your elderly neighbor's lawn once a week. (A little exercise is always good!)

- If you like to cook or bake, prepare a meal for a friend who has just had a baby or for someone you know who is being challenged. (You're making your dinner anyhow ... now you have meals for more!)

- Pick one person a week you've lost touch with and call them. (You may be the lifeline they need ... and they could be one for you.)

- If you have young children or grandchildren, take them to visit a nursing home. Little children always bring smiles to elders. (And leave it to a child to find ways to do more for them!)

Giving of yourself raises you up, along with those whose lives you've touched. When you give and expect nothing in return, problems you have no longer carry the weight they once did. And when your load is lighter ... so is your spirit!

Live Each Day

We love our weekends. We don't have to work, and we have time with others we want to be with. Loving the weekends is one thing ... living for them is another.

Living for two-sevenths of our time here on earth just isn't good enough. We have a chance to embrace every day and to enjoy each moment.

How about you? Are you focused on the good in your life every day? Try this very **Simple Step** to start your day off right:

- Every morning, get up a few minutes early.

- As you sit and drink your favorite wake-up beverage, look around at your surroundings.

- Count up all the blessings you see.

- Give thanks.

Carpe diem! Seize the Day!

About the Author

When Cheryl first started writing a blog in 2009, she was an out-of-work, out-of-shape, over-fifty corporate executive collecting unemployment, questioning her own worth, dealing with her husband Jack's scary health diagnoses and beating herself up for the stupid financial mistakes she had made. Is that enough baggage?

After months of writing daily, Cheryl started posting her thoughts on Facebook. She knew she wasn't alone in her challenges . . . but what she discovered was just how many people were dealing with some major issue in their lives. Now they know they're not alone either. Cheryl is passionate about helping others, and **Simple Steps** . . . **Real Change** was born from that passion.

Jack and Cheryl now live in Portland, Oregon with their dog, CJ, and their cats. They love exploring the mountains, ocean and small towns of the Pacific Northwest. Cheryl continues to write a daily blog and share inspirational messages on the **Simple Steps** . . . **Real Change** website and on the Facebook page.

Other Works By

Kenny Brixey: ***No Excuses… No Limits… Just Results.***
http://www.unlimitedreality.net/

Brent Carey: *Empower Radio.* http://www.empoweradio.com/

Paul S. Boynton: ***Begin With Yes***. http://www.beginwithyes.com/

Mary Cimiluca and Noetic Films: ***Viktor & I:*** An Alexander Vesely
Film. http://www.viktorandimovie.com/

Made in the USA
Monee, IL
20 November 2020

48713138R00132